Breakfast at Nine, Tea at Four

Favorite Recipes from Cape May's Mainstay Inn

Sue Carroll

Breakfast at Nine, Tea at Four: Favorite Recipes from Cape May's Mainstay Inn

Cataloguing in Publication Data
Carroll, Sue, 1946–
Breakfast at nine, tea at four : favorite recipes from
Cape May's Mainstay Inn

Includes index.
ISBN 1-896511-08-2

1. Breakfasts. 2. Afternoon teas. 3. Mainstay Inn.
I. Title.

TX715.C376 1997 641.5'2 C97-900408-X

Back cover photography by (left to right) George W. Gardner (Mainstay sweets and savories) and Tom Carroll (Tropical Fruit with Mango Sauce; the Mainstay in full bloom).
Front and back cover design by Shari Blaukopf. Front cover line drawing by Bob Bates.
Book design by Marcy Claman. Copy editing by Jane Broderick. Indexing by Christine Jacobs.

Verses from "Humors of Cape May" by Edward F. Underhill, 1871.
Vintage Victorian illustrations from the Dover Electronic Pictorial and Design Series.

10 9 8 7 6 5 4 3 2 1

Printed in Canada.

Callawind Publications Inc.
3383 Sources Boulevard, Suite 205, Dollard-des-Ormeaux, Quebec H9B 1Z8 Canada
2083 Hempstead Turnpike, Suite 355, East Meadow, New York 11554-1730 USA
http://www.callawind.com e-mail: info@callawind.com

Bill of Fare

A Measure of Thanks

First, I would like to thank my parents, who gave my sister and me free rein in the kitchen from an early age.

I also thank my excellent staff — Diane Clark, Kathy Moore, Beth Stone, and Jill Turner — who tested recipes and proofread my manuscript and who have lifted many of the burdens of innkeeping from my shoulders.

It was our guests who first inspired me to publish a collection of my favorite recipes. I thank them for that and for their patronage, which has made it possible for us to continue running the Mainstay Inn.

I must also thank my wonderful husband, Tom, for not grumbling when I was too busy working on this cookbook to make anything for him to eat.

Lastly, I offer heartfelt thanks to my publisher, Marcy Claman, who conceived the idea of this cookbook and who helped me every step of the way.

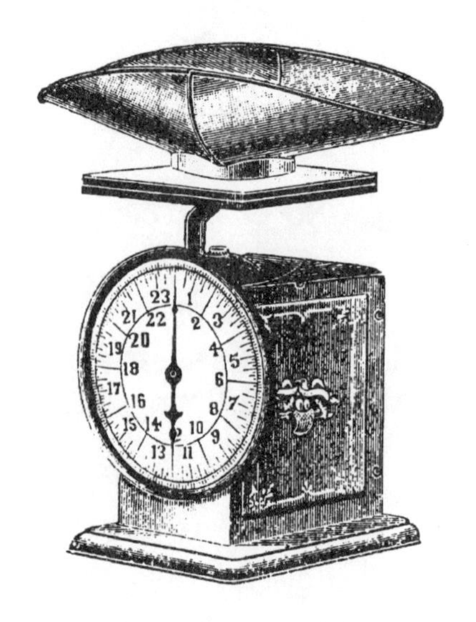

Introduction

Serving both breakfast and afternoon tea has added a unique dimension to the Mainstay Inn. It posed an interesting challenge to my husband, Tom Carroll, and me as innkeepers, but for two decades now our delicious breakfast dishes and afternoon sweets and savories have delighted our guests. Their frequent requests for recipes tell us so — they scribble ingredients on note cards just as the dishes are being cleared away, often kindly offering their own favorites in exchange.

Keen interest in our breakfast menus in particular has led to this collection of recipes from numerous sources. My staff and I are constantly experimenting in the kitchen to come up with flavorful creations, with simplicity as the keynote. In addition, many recipes have been contributed by our guests, while other favorites originate from relatives and friends from all over the country.

All are perfectly suitable for Sunday brunch entertaining. Preparation is easy and can be done the evening before, freeing the host and hostess for conversation. Tom and I planned our menus with this in mind: we make it a point to join our Mainstay guests for breakfast.

Afternoon tea is served daily at the Mainstay. On Tuesdays, Thursdays, Saturdays, and Sundays it follows our four o'clock house tour, which is open to the public. After learning about the colorful history of the inn, our tour visitors join our overnight guests for afternoon refreshments.

For most of the year we serve tea in the dining room. The mood is informal, though, and, if weather permits, guests take their hot beverage and a few tasty morsels out to the veranda, find a rocker, and just relax. In summer we serve iced tea with an assortment of tea cookies, confections, dainty sandwiches, and delicious spreads.

What can't be shared in any cookbook is the warmth that's kindled at our table. Strangers are no more. Age and occupation become insignificant. There's real communication among people — much to our pleasure. I hope the recipes I've collected here will convey some of this friendliness to you. Happy cooking.

— *Sue Carroll*

History of the Mainstay Inn

The building now known as the Mainstay Inn has always caused passers-by to stop in their tracks. Even in Cape May, a National Historic Landmark community famous for its hundreds of restored Victorian homes, the Mainstay stands out.

Ringed by flower beds and framed by a picket fence, the cream-colored inn features an impressive pillared façade, a vast three-sided veranda lined with wooden rocking chairs, and an ornately bracketed cupola.

As newcomers to Cape May in 1969, my husband, Tom, and I loved to stroll past this beautiful structure and dream about one day owning it.

A writer for the local newspaper was equally enchanted in 1872, upon completion of the building: "It is symmetrical in its proportions, airy and cheerful in its appointments, and finished in that unpretentious elegance so foreign to mansions of the shoddy order."

The Mainstay Inn retains all of its period elegance, but behind the graceful façade lies a racy past. It was built by a pair of wealthy gamblers as a sumptuous private club for gentlemen to drink, smoke cigars, talk politics, and above all gamble. No ladies were permitted beyond the spacious veranda, where they were welcome to take tea. The Clubhouse, as it was known, flourished until the turn of the century, when the City of Cape May voted to outlaw the sale of alcohol and the State of New Jersey declared gambling illegal.

The mansion was then sold for a third of its original cost and passed more respectable days as the summer residence of a wealthy Philadelphia family, then as the home of a retired Baptist minister. Only minor changes were made and its architectural integrity was retained.

When, in 1976, we were at last able to acquire our dream house, we found the building much as it had been when the gamblers reveled in its Victorian splendor. The bedrooms were furnished with elaborate Renaissance-style beds and dressers, small pulleys were fixed to the ceilings so that mosquito nets could be lowered over

the beds (the mosquito nets were there too, though in tatters), and chamber pots were still to be found under the beds, resting on little trays with rollers.

The public rooms were unchanged as well. The 14-foot ceilings were embellished with ornate plaster medallions from which hung elaborate gas chandeliers. The original mirrors — one 13 feet high — were still in place, as were marble-topped servers and a dining table that could seat more than a dozen people.

However, we found evidence of the worst of 19th-century life, as well as the best. There had never been a heating system of any kind, bathrooms were few and poorly functioning, and the kitchen was hopelessly antiquated. The interior of the building was dark and dingy, having been painted only once since 1872.

During the winter of 1976–77 we applied more than 50 gallons of paint to the rooms and corridors and we stitched 400 yards of lace to make window coverings. We combed antique shops and auction houses all over the East for additions to the original furnishings. We used a mile of copper pipe for the heating system.

Our goal was to have our guests experience only the best of 19th-century life — we wanted our inn to have the character of an historic structure but the atmosphere and comfort of a family home.

Over the years we have made many improvements to the Mainstay Inn, even acquiring two additional historic buildings in the process. Throughout it all we have found great enjoyment in recreating the gracious style in which our Victorian ancestors spent their leisure time in fashionable Cape May.

Clattering of the dishes,
Rattling knives and forks,
Jingling of the glasses,
Popping of the corks,
Draining of the bottles,
Stowing food away,
Don't we have a jolly time
In dining at Cape May?

Fruit Dishes

Broiled Grapefruit

2 medium grapefruits
6 tablespoons brown sugar
2 tablespoons butter
4 maraschino cherries

Halve the grapefruits and loosen the sections with a grapefruit knife. Sprinkle with the sugar and dot with the butter.

Place on a baking sheet and broil for 2 – 3 minutes or until the sugar is caramelized. Top each grapefruit half with a cherry.

Serve warm.

Yield: 4 servings

Hot Fruit Compote

2 (16-ounce) cans sliced peaches
2 (16-ounce) cans sliced pears
1 (20-ounce) can pineapple chunks
1 (16½-ounce) can dark, sweet pitted cherries
3 medium bananas, sliced (2 cups)
¾ cup brown sugar
⅓ cup butter (⅙ pound)
1 (16-ounce) can applesauce
1 cup pecan halves

Preheat the oven to 300°F. Grease a 13 x 9 x 2-inch glass baking dish.

Drain well the canned peaches, pears, pineapple, and cherries. Combine these fruits with the banana slices and place in the prepared baking dish.

Place the sugar, butter, and applesauce in a saucepan and heat thoroughly, stirring occasionally.

Spoon the applesauce mixture over the fruit. Arrange the pecan halves on top and bake for 60 minutes.

Serve hot.

Yield: 8 servings

Spiced Fruit Compote

4 medium pears, peeled, cored, and sliced (4 cups)
4 medium apples, peeled, cored, and sliced (4 cups)
1 (20-ounce) can pineapple bits, drained
1 cup whole-berry cranberry sauce
¼ teaspoon ground cinnamon
½ teaspoon ground cloves
½ teaspoon ground allspice

Preheat the oven to 350°F.

Layer the pear and apple slices in a shallow 2-quart glass casserole. Combine the pineapple, cranberry sauce, cinnamon, cloves, and allspice. Spoon this over the pear and apple slices.

Bake for 30 minutes or until the fruit is soft.

Serve warm.

Yield: 8 servings

Hot Cranberry-Apple Compote

3 cups peeled and chopped tart apple (3 medium)
2 cups fresh cranberries (½ pound)
2 teaspoons lemon juice
1 cup granulated sugar
1⅓ cups quick-cooking rolled oats
⅓ cup light brown sugar
1 teaspoon ground cinnamon
½ cup butter (¼ pound)

Preheat the oven to 350°F. Lightly grease a 2-quart glass casserole.

Combine the apple, cranberries, and lemon juice in the prepared casserole. Toss well. Distribute the granulated sugar evenly over the fruit.

Combine the rolled oats, brown sugar, cinnamon, and butter, mixing well. Sprinkle this over the layer of sugar.

Bake for 60 minutes or until lightly browned.

Serve hot.

Yield: 8 servings

Baked Bananas

8 medium slightly underripe bananas, sliced (5 cups)
¼ cup lemon juice
1 cup honey
4 strips bacon, cooked and crumbled

Preheat the oven to 350°F. Grease a shallow 1½-quart glass baking dish.

Place the banana slices in the prepared baking dish. Pour the lemon juice, then the honey, over the banana slices.

Bake for 30 minutes and sprinkle with the bacon.

Serve warm.

Yield: 8 servings

Baked Pineapple

½ cup butter (¼ pound)
¾ cup sugar
4 eggs
1 (17¼-ounce) can crushed pineapple, drained
5 slices bread, cut into 1-inch cubes

Preheat the oven to 350°F. Grease an 8-inch-square glass baking dish.

Cream the butter and sugar. Add the eggs and beat well. Fold in the pineapple and the bread cubes.

Turn into the prepared baking dish and bake for 45 minutes or until browned.

Serve warm.

Yield: 4 servings

Banana-Pineapple Crisp

3 medium ripe bananas, sliced ½-inch thick (2 cups)
1 (20-ounce) can pineapple chunks, drained, reserving ¼ cup juice
2 tablespoons apricot preserves

TOPPING
½ cup large-flake rolled oats
½ cup light brown sugar
¼ cup all-purpose flour
¼ cup sweetened flaked coconut
¼ cup butter, cut into small pieces (⅛ pound)

Preheat the oven to 400°F.

Gently mix the banana and pineapple in a shallow 1½-quart glass baking dish. Stir the apricot preserves into the ¼ cup of reserved pineapple juice and pour this over the fruit mixture.

To prepare the topping, mix the rolled oats, sugar, flour, and coconut in a medium bowl. Cut in the butter with a pastry blender or two knives until the mixture is crumbly. Sprinkle over the fruit mixture.

Bake for 15 – 20 minutes or until the topping is lightly browned and the juices bubble up.

Serve hot.

Yield:* 6 *servings

Speedy Cranberry Pears

4 canned pear halves, drained, reserving ¼ cup juice
4 teaspoons butter
4 tablespoons commercial cranberry-orange relish

Preheat the oven to 350°F.

Pour the reserved pear juice into an 8-inch-square glass baking dish and top with the pear halves. Place 1 teaspoon of the butter in the hollow of each pear half and top with 1 tablespoon of the relish.

Bake for 15 minutes or until heated through.

Serve warm.

Yield: 4 servings

Poached Apples

1½ cups orange juice
2 teaspoons grated orange zest
¼ cup sugar
½ teaspoon ground cinnamon
4 medium apples, cored and quartered but not peeled

Mix the orange juice, orange zest, sugar, and cinnamon in a saucepan. Add the apple and simmer for 15 – 20 minutes or until soft.

Serve warm or cold.

Yield:* *8 servings

Poached Pears with Brandied Cranberries

Pears
2 cups cranberry juice
2 tablespoons brown sugar
½ teaspoon ground cinnamon
½ teaspoon ground nutmeg
4 firm medium pears, peeled, cored, and halved

Brandied Cranberries
1½ (12-ounce) packages fresh cranberries (18 ounces total)
1½ cups sugar
¼ cup brandy

First, prepare the pears. In a saucepan, bring the cranberry juice, sugar, cinnamon, and nutmeg to a boil. Add the pear halves and simmer for 30 minutes. Refrigerate for 60 minutes or until thoroughly chilled.

Next, make the brandied cranberries. Preheat the oven to 350°F. Lightly grease a 15 x 10 x 1-inch jelly roll pan.

Arrange the cranberries in a single layer in the prepared pan. Top with the sugar. Cover tightly with foil and bake for 45 minutes. Spoon into a bowl and add the brandy, tossing to combine. Refrigerate for 60 minutes or until thoroughly chilled.

Serve the chilled cranberries over the chilled pears.

Yield: 8 servings

Ginger-Glazed Fruit

3 tablespoons sugar
2 teaspoons cornstarch
½ cup apple juice
1 teaspoon lemon juice
½ teaspoon ground ginger
5 cups fresh fruit (such as cantaloupe, pineapple, apple, strawberries, blueberries)

In a medium saucepan, combine the sugar and cornstarch. Stir in the apple juice, lemon juice, and ginger. Cook over medium heat, stirring constantly, until the mixture comes to a full boil and is slightly thickened. Cool completely.

Place the fruit in a large serving bowl. Add the glaze and stir gently to coat.

Serve chilled or at room temperature.

***Yield:** 6 – 8 servings*

Tropical Fruit with Mango Sauce

2 cups peeled, diced kiwi (6 large)
2 cups peeled, seeded, and diced papaya (2 medium)
2 medium bananas, sliced (1½ cups)
1 cup drained canned pineapple bits (8 ounces)
2 tablespoons lime juice

MANGO SAUCE
2 mangos, peeled, seeded, and diced (2 cups)
3 tablespoons honey
2 tablespoons lemon juice

Toss the kiwi, papaya, banana, and pineapple with the lime juice.

In a food processor, purée the mango with the honey and lemon juice. Spoon the mango sauce over the fruit.

Serve cold.

Yield: 8 servings; 2 cups of mango sauce

Frozen Fruit Cup

4 medium bananas, mashed (2½ cups)
1 cup fresh blueberries, or frozen, thawed (½ pint)
1 (10-ounce) package frozen strawberries, thawed
1 (16-ounce) can crushed pineapple, undrained
2 cups ginger ale
1 (6-ounce) can frozen orange juice concentrate, thawed
1 (6-ounce) can frozen lemonade concentrate, thawed

Place all the ingredients in a large pitcher and stir. Pour into individual freezer-proof cups and freeze.

Remove from the freezer 30 minutes before serving, to partially defrost.

Yield: 8 servings

Fruit Kabobs

¼ cup lemon juice
¼ cup orange juice
1 tablespoon sugar
1 cup fresh strawberries (½ pint)
1 cup seedless grapes (¼ pound)
1 cup cantaloupe balls (½ medium)
1 medium banana, sliced ¾-inch thick (½ cup)
1 cup lemon yogurt

Combine the lemon juice, orange juice, and sugar in a large bowl. Add the strawberries, grapes, cantaloupe, and banana, tossing to combine. Refrigerate for 2 hours.

Arrange the fruit on eight small skewers and serve cold, with the lemon yogurt.

Yield: 8 servings

Fruit Pizza

FILLING
1 (14-ounce) can sweetened condensed milk
½ cup sour cream
¼ cup lemon juice
1 teaspoon vanilla

DOUGH
½ cup softened butter (¼ pound)
¼ cup brown sugar
1 cup all-purpose flour
¼ cup quick-cooking rolled oats
¼ cup finely chopped walnuts

GLAZE
½ cup apricot preserves
2 tablespoons brandy
4 cups thinly sliced fresh fruit (such as kiwis, strawberries, bananas)

To make the filling, mix the milk, sour cream, lemon juice, and vanilla. Refrigerate for at least 30 minutes.

Preheat the oven to 375°F. Lightly oil a 12-inch pizza pan.

To make the dough, beat the butter and sugar until fluffy. Mix in the flour, rolled oats, and walnuts.

Place the dough on the prepared pizza pan and press it into a circle, forming a rim around the edge. Prick with a fork and bake for 10 – 12 minutes. Cool.

To make the glaze, melt the apricot preserves in a small saucepan over low heat. Add the brandy and mix. Strain.

Spoon the chilled filling over the cooled crust. Arrange the fruit slices in a circular pattern over the filling. Brush the apricot glaze over the fruit. Cover and refrigerate for 60 minutes.

Serve cold, cut into wedges.

Yield: 8 servings

Dreamsicle Oranges

2 cups water
2 cups sugar
2 teaspoons vanilla
6 navel oranges, peeled and thinly sliced, reserving the peel from one orange

Combine the water and sugar in a saucepan and boil for 5 minutes. Stir in the vanilla. Add the orange peel and boil for 5 more minutes. Remove from heat and allow to cool for 30 minutes.

Arrange the orange slices on a flat serving dish. Remove the peel from the syrup and discard. Pour the syrup over the orange slices. Cover and refrigerate for 60 minutes.

Serve chilled or at room temperature.

Yield: 8 servings

Creamy Pineapple

2 cups sour cream
1 (17¼-ounce) can crushed pineapple, drained
1 medium pineapple, cut into 8 slices
1 (11-ounce) can mandarin orange sections

Mix the sour cream and pineapple and spoon on top of the pineapple slices. Top with the orange sections.

Serve cold.

Yield: 8 servings

Heavenly Bananas

½ cup sour cream
2 tablespoons sugar
1 tablespoon orange juice
1 teaspoon grated orange zest
2 medium bananas, sliced (1½ cups)
1 cup sliced fresh strawberries (½ pint)

Combine the sour cream, sugar, orange juice, and orange zest. Blend well. Fold in the banana slices and refrigerate for 60 minutes.

When chilled, top with the strawberry slices.

Serve cold.

***Yield:** 6 servings*

Banana-Blueberry Delight

1 cup sour cream
½ cup brown sugar
1 teaspoon vanilla
2 large bananas, sliced (2 cups)
2 cups fresh blueberries (1 pint)

Combine the sour cream, sugar, and vanilla. Carefully fold in the banana and 1½ cups of the blueberries. Refrigerate for 30 minutes.

Serve cold, topped with the reserved ½ cup of blueberries.

Yield:* *6 servings

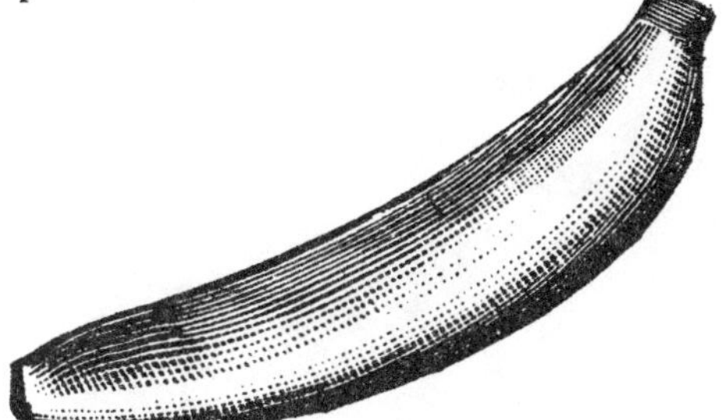

Minted Melon

⅓ cup sugar
⅓ cup lemon juice
2 tablespoons finely chopped fresh mint
2 cups cantaloupe balls (1 medium)
2 cups honeydew melon balls (½ medium)

Combine the sugar and lemon juice. Add the mint. Pour this over the cantaloupe and melon balls and refrigerate for 60 minutes.

Serve cold.

Yield: 4 servings

St. Paddy's Day Fruit Medley

4 large kiwis, peeled and sliced (1⅓ cups)
2 Granny Smith apples, cored and sliced but not peeled (2 cups)
1 cup seedless green grapes (¼ pound)
1 cup honeydew melon balls (¼ medium)
Green leaf lettuce

Honey-Lime Dressing
1 (16-ounce) container plain yogurt
2 tablespoons honey
2 teaspoons grated lime zest

Arrange the kiwi slices, apple slices, grapes, and melon balls on the lettuce leaves.

To make the dressing, combine the yogurt, honey, and lime zest. Refrigerate for 60 minutes.

Drizzle the dressing over the fruit and serve cold.

Yield: 6 servings

Peach and Vanilla Yogurt Parfait

PEACH SAUCE
2 cups peeled, pitted, and crushed peaches (6 medium)
½ cup sugar
½ cup orange juice
2 teaspoons lemon juice
1 teaspoon vanilla

1 (32-ounce) container low-fat vanilla yogurt
6 – 8 maraschino cherries or strawberries

First, make the sauce. Mix the peaches, sugar, and orange juice in a saucepan. Simmer, uncovered, for 15 minutes. Remove from heat and stir in the lemon juice and vanilla. Chill.

To make the parfait, place a few tablespoons of yogurt in a small parfait glass. Place a layer of chilled peach sauce over the yogurt. Repeat these steps once or twice more, until the last peach layer reaches the top of the glass. Top with a cherry.

Note: Any leftover peach sauce can be served warm over pancakes, waffles, or ice cream.

***Yield:** 6 – 8 servings; 2½ cups of peach sauce*

Specialties of the House

Fruited Oatmeal

1/3 cup raisins
2/3 cup large-flake rolled oats
1 tablespoon frozen orange juice concentrate, thawed
1/4 teaspoon ground cinnamon
1 cup unpeeled chopped apple (1 medium)
1/8 teaspoon maple extract

In a medium saucepan, bring the raisins to a boil in 2 cups of water. Mix in the rolled oats, orange juice concentrate, and cinnamon. Cover. Reduce heat and simmer for 8 – 10 minutes.

Let stand for 5 minutes. Stir in the chopped apple and the maple extract.

Serve hot.

Yield: 5 servings

Mainstay French Toast with Spicy Apple Syrup

The French toast must be prepared the night before, then baked just before serving time.

½ cup butter (¼ pound)
1 cup brown sugar
2 tablespoons corn syrup
2 medium tart apples, peeled, cored, and sliced (2 cups)
1 (1-pound) loaf French bread, cut into 12 – 14 (1-inch) slices
5 eggs
1½ cups milk
1 teaspoon vanilla

SPICY APPLE SYRUP
1 (10-ounce) jar apple jelly
1 cup applesauce
½ teaspoon ground cinnamon
⅛ teaspoon ground cloves
Dash of salt

Heat the butter, sugar, and corn syrup in a saucepan until the mixture is syrupy. Pour into an ungreased 13 x 9 x 2-inch glass baking dish. Cover with the apple, then the bread.

Whisk together the eggs, milk, and vanilla and pour the mixture over the bread. Cover and refrigerate for at least 8 hours, or overnight.

Preheat the oven to 350°F and bake, uncovered, for 40 minutes or until lightly browned.

Meanwhile, make the syrup. Combine all the ingredients in a small saucepan. Cook over medium heat, stirring constantly, until the jelly is melted and the syrup is hot.

Separate the French toast slices with a knife and serve immediately, with the warm syrup.

Yield: 6 – 8 servings; 1½ cups of apple syrup

Orange French Toast

This dish must be prepared the night before, then baked just before serving time.

5 eggs
⅔ cup heavy whipping cream
⅓ cup orange-flavored liqueur
2 tablespoons sugar
¼ cup fresh orange juice
1 tablespoon grated orange zest
1 teaspoon ground cinnamon
2 tablespoons butter, melted
1 (1-pound) loaf French bread, cut into 12 – 14 (1-inch) slices
Maple syrup, warmed
Orange slices

Whisk the eggs and cream until very light and frothy. Add the liqueur, sugar, orange juice, orange zest, and cinnamon, blending well.

Cover the bottom of a 13 x 9 x 2-inch glass baking dish with the melted butter. Arrange the bread slices over the bottom of the dish. Pour the egg mixture evenly over the bread.

Cover and refrigerate for at least 8 hours, or overnight.

Preheat the oven to 350°F. Bake for 30 minutes or until the bread is lightly browned.

Separate the French toast slices with a knife. Serve warm with the warmed maple syrup, garnished with the orange slices.

***Yield:** 6 – 8 servings*

Eggnog French Toast with Cranberry Syrup

The French toast must be prepared the night before, then baked just before serving time.

4 ounces softened cream cheese
¼ cup dried cranberries (1 ounce)
1 (1-pound) loaf French bread, cut into 12 – 14 (1-inch) slices
2½ cups half-and-half
6 tablespoons butter, melted
8 eggs
¼ teaspoon ground nutmeg
¼ cup sugar
1 teaspoon vanilla
1 teaspoon rum extract

Cranberry Syrup
1 cup frozen raspberry-cranberry juice concentrate, thawed
1 cup whole-berry cranberry sauce
⅓ cup sugar
1 tablespoon cornstarch

Grease a 13 x 9 x 2-inch glass baking dish.

In a food processor, combine the cream cheese and cranberries. Cut part way through each slice of bread to form a pocket. Fill with the cheese mixture and arrange in the baking dish.

In a large bowl, whisk the cream, butter, eggs, nutmeg, sugar, vanilla, and rum extract. Pour evenly over the bread slices. Cover and refrigerate for at least 8 hours, or overnight, then preheat the oven to 350°F and bake for 30 minutes or until golden brown.

Meanwhile, make the syrup. Combine all the ingredients in a small saucepan. Whisk over medium-low heat until dissolved and slightly thickened.

Separate the French toast slices with a knife and serve immediately, with the cranberry syrup.

***Yield:** 6 – 8 servings; 2 cups of cranberry syrup*

Stuffed French Toast with Strawberry Sauce

The French toast must be prepared the night before, then baked just before serving time.

8 ounces cream cheese
1 (1½-pound) loaf firm white bread, cut into 16 (1-inch) slices
10 eggs
1½ cups half-and-half
¼ cup maple syrup
½ cup butter, melted (¼ pound)

Strawberry Sauce
2 cups sliced fresh strawberries (1 pint)
2 cups strawberry preserves

Grease a 13 x 9 x 2-inch glass baking dish.

Spread the cream cheese over half the bread slices. Cover with the remaining slices to make sandwiches. Remove the crusts and cut into 1-inch cubes. Place in the prepared baking dish.

Mix the eggs, cream, maple syrup, and melted butter until well blended. Pour evenly over the bread; press the bread down until it soaks up the egg mixture. Cover and refrigerate for at least 8 hours, or overnight.

Preheat the oven to 350°F and bake for 40 – 50 minutes or until lightly browned.

Meanwhile, make the sauce. Heat the strawberries and strawberry preserves in a saucepan, stirring gently, until the preserves have melted.

Cut the French toast into squares and serve warm, with the strawberry sauce.

Yield: 8 – 10 servings; 3½ cups of strawberry sauce

Herb Frittata

2 tablespoons margarine
1 cup peeled, sliced zucchini (1 small)
⅓ cup chopped scallions
1 (5-ounce) container soft cream cheese with herbs and garlic
¼ cup milk
6 eggs, beaten
2 cups frozen hash brown potatoes, thawed
¼ teaspoon salt
⅛ teaspoon pepper
1 cup grated Monterey Jack cheese (4 ounces)

Preheat the oven to 350°F.

Melt the margarine in a 10-inch ovenproof frying pan and sauté the zucchini and scallions.

In a medium bowl, stir the cream cheese and milk until blended. Add the eggs, potato, salt, and pepper, mixing well. Turn the mixture into the frying pan with the zucchini and scallions.

Bake for 25 – 30 minutes or until set.

Top with the Monterey Jack cheese and let stand for 5 minutes or until the cheese is melted.

Cut into wedges and serve immediately.

Yield: 8 servings

Western Oven Omelet

¾ cup mild salsa
1 cup chopped artichoke hearts
¼ cup grated Parmesan cheese (1 ounce)
1 cup grated Monterey Jack cheese (4 ounces)
1 cup grated sharp Cheddar cheese (4 ounces)
6 eggs
1 cup sour cream

Preheat the oven to 350°F. Grease a 10-inch pie plate.

Spread the salsa in the bottom of the prepared pie plate. Distribute the chopped artichoke hearts evenly over the salsa. Sprinkle with the Parmesan cheese, then the Monterey Jack, then the Cheddar.

Beat the eggs with the sour cream and spread over the cheese.

Bake for 30 minutes or until set.

Cut into wedges and serve immediately.

***Yield:** 6 servings*

Baked Swiss Cheese Omelet

2 cups grated Swiss cheese (8 ounces)
¼ cup butter (⅛ pound)
1½ teaspoons powdered mustard
½ teaspoon salt
Dash of pepper
1 cup heavy whipping cream
12 eggs, lightly beaten

Preheat the oven to 325°F. Grease a 13 x 9 x 2-inch glass baking dish.

Spread the cheese over the bottom of the prepared baking dish. Dot with the butter.

Stir the powdered mustard, salt, and pepper into the cream and pour half of this mixture over the cheese. Add the beaten eggs. Pour the remainder of the cream mixture on top.

Bake for 30 minutes or until set.

Cut into squares and serve warm.

Yield: 8 servings

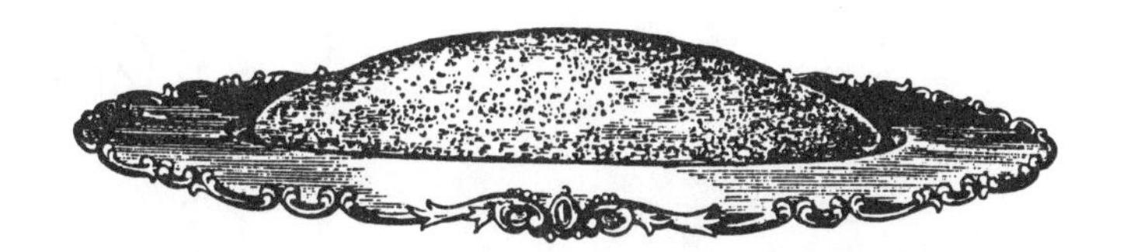

Creamy Scrambled Eggs

5 tablespoons milk
12 eggs, well beaten
1 tablespoon margarine
1 cup sour cream
4 ounces cream cheese
2 tablespoons chopped fresh parsley
1 teaspoon seasoned salt

Preheat the oven to 325°F. Grease a 13 x 9 x 2-inch glass baking dish.

Combine the milk with the beaten eggs. Melt the margarine in a large frying pan over low heat and scramble the eggs until firm but moist.

Mix the sour cream, cream cheese, parsley, and seasoned salt. Fold gently into the scrambled egg.

Turn the mixture into the prepared baking dish and bake for 30 minutes or until piping hot.

Serve immediately.

Yield: 8 servings

Scrambled Eggs for a Crowd

¼ cup butter (⅛ pound)
12 eggs
1⅓ cups milk
2 tablespoons all-purpose flour
1 tablespoon chopped fresh parsley
1 teaspoon salt
⅛ teaspoon pepper

Melt the butter in a large frying pan over low heat.

Place the eggs, milk, flour, parsley, salt, and pepper in a large bowl and beat until smooth and well blended. Turn into the frying pan.

Stir from the edge toward the center, allowing the uncooked egg in the center to flow to the edge. Continue stirring until all the egg has been cooked and the mixture is creamy.

Serve immediately.

Note: Scrambled eggs may be kept warm for up to 2 hours in a chafing dish or an oven set at 200°F.

Yield: 8 servings

Baked Eggs with Leeks and Tarragon

The first part of this recipe can be made a day in advance.

4 tablespoons butter (1/8 pound)
3 large leeks (white and pale green parts only), coarsely chopped
1½ cups grated Jarlsberg cheese (6 ounces)
½ cup freshly grated Parmesan cheese (2 ounces)
8 eggs
2 cups heavy whipping cream
2 tablespoons chopped fresh tarragon, or 1 teaspoon dried
½ teaspoon salt
¼ teaspoon freshly ground pepper
Fresh tarragon sprigs

Preheat the oven to 375°F. Grease a 13 x 9 x 2-inch glass baking dish with 1 tablespoon of the butter.

Melt the remaining 3 tablespoons of butter in a large, heavy frying pan over medium-high heat. Sauté the leeks for 5 minutes or until tender. Spread in the bottom of the prepared dish. (If preparing this part of the recipe a day ahead, cover and refrigerate.)

Combine the Jarlsberg and Parmesan cheeses in a bowl. Spread all but ½ cup of the mixture over the leeks.

Whisk the eggs, cream, chopped tarragon, salt, and pepper in a large bowl. Pour this over the leeks.

Bake for 30 minutes or until golden brown and set in the center. Sprinkle with the remaining ½ cup of cheese and bake for another 5 minutes or until melted.

Garnish with the tarragon sprigs and cut into squares. Serve warm.

Yield: 8 servings

Savory Baked Eggs

1 (10-ounce) package frozen ready-to-bake puff pastry shells (6 shells)
6 eggs, at room temperature
3 tablespoons chopped scallions
1 cup grated sharp Cheddar cheese (4 ounces)
3 tablespoons chopped fresh parsley
3 tablespoons chopped fresh basil

Prepare the pastry shells according to the package directions but bake for only 20 minutes. Cool. Remove the tops and the soft dough inside.

Preheat the oven to 350°F. Grease a 13 x 9 x 2-inch glass baking dish.

Place the baked pastry shells in the prepared baking dish. Carefully break an egg into each and bake for 20 minutes or until the eggs are set.

Remove from the oven and sprinkle with the scallions and the cheese. Return to the oven and bake just until the cheese has melted. Sprinkle with the parsley and basil and serve immediately.

Yield: 6 servings

California Egg Puff

10 eggs
½ cup all-purpose flour
1 teaspoon baking powder
½ teaspoon salt
4 cups grated Monterey Jack cheese (1 pound)
½ cup butter, melted (¼ pound)
1 (4-ounce) can green chilies, diced
2 cups creamed cottage cheese

Preheat the oven to 350°F. Grease a 13 x 9 x 2-inch glass baking dish.

Beat the eggs until light and frothy. Add the flour, baking powder, salt, Monterey Jack cheese, melted butter, chilies, and cottage cheese. Stir until well blended.

Turn into the prepared baking dish and bake for 25 – 30 minutes or until puffed up and slightly browned.

Cut into squares and serve hot.

Yield: 8 servings

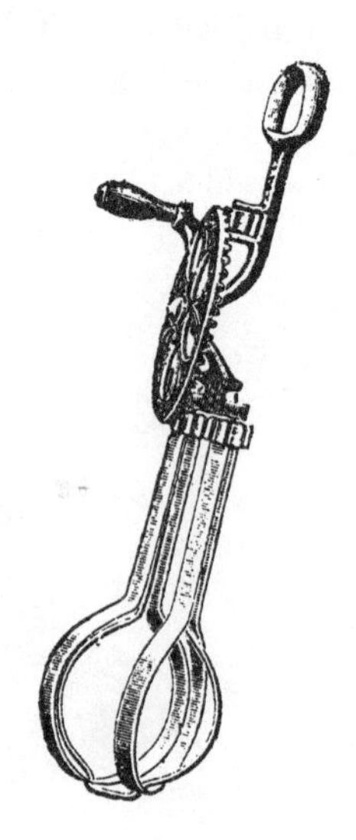

Breakfast Soufflé

9 slices bread, cubed
2 cups grated sharp Cheddar cheese (8 ounces)
3 eggs
2 cups milk
1 teaspoon salt
½ teaspoon Worcestershire sauce
½ teaspoon Tabasco sauce
½ teaspoon powdered mustard
¼ teaspoon dried thyme

Grease a 13 x 9 x 2-inch glass baking dish.

Alternate layers of the bread and the cheese in the prepared baking dish.

Beat the eggs, milk, salt, Worcestershire sauce, Tabasco sauce, powdered mustard, and thyme and pour the mixture over the bread and cheese. Let stand at least 30 minutes.

Preheat the oven to 300°F and bake for 60 minutes or until puffed up and golden.

Cut into squares and serve warm.

Yield: 8 servings

Individual Orange Soufflés

Both the egg yolk mixture and the egg white mixture in this recipe can be made in advance. Simply cover and refrigerate for up to 12 hours, then beat just before mixing with the other ingredients. Prepare the orange sauce first. Otherwise, the egg whites might deflate a bit while you're cooking the sauce.

ORANGE SAUCE
¾ cup orange juice
2 tablespoons butter
2 tablespoons brown sugar
1 tablespoon cornstarch

SOUFFLÉS
4 tablespoons sugar
5 eggs, separated
2 tablespoons all-purpose flour
1 tablespoon grated orange zest

To prepare the orange sauce, cook the orange juice, butter, brown sugar, and cornstarch in a small saucepan, stirring, over medium heat for 3 – 5 minutes or until the butter is melted and the sauce is heated through and slightly thickened. Keep warm over low heat.

Next, prepare the soufflés. Preheat the oven to 375°F. Grease six (5-ounce) soufflé dishes or custard cups. Sprinkle with 2 tablespoons of sugar; shake out any excess. Place 1 tablespoon of the orange sauce in the bottom of each soufflé dish, reserving the remaining sauce.

Whisk the egg yolks, flour, and orange zest in a large bowl until well blended.

Beat the egg whites and the remaining 2 tablespoons of sugar in a medium bowl with an electric mixer on high speed for 3 – 5 minutes or until soft peaks form.

Fold the egg white mixture into the yolk mixture. Divide this mixture equally into the soufflé dishes.

Place the dishes in a baking pan and bake for 15 – 20 minutes or until golden brown.

Serve immediately, with the reserved warm orange sauce.

Yield: 6 servings; 1 cup of orange sauce

Blintz Soufflé with Fruit Sauce

Filling

8 ounces cream cheese
2 cups ricotta cheese
2 egg yolks
1 tablespoon sugar
1 teaspoon vanilla

Batter

½ cup softened butter (¼ pound)
⅓ cup sugar
6 eggs
1 cup all-purpose flour
2 teaspoons baking powder
1½ cups sour cream
½ cup orange juice

Fruit Sauce

1 (8-ounce) jar seedless raspberry jam
1 cup fresh blueberries (½ pint)
1 cup sliced fresh strawberries (½ pint)

Preheat the oven to 350°F. Grease a 13 x 9 x 2-inch glass baking dish.

First, prepare the filling. In a small bowl, beat the cream cheese until smooth. Add the ricotta cheese, egg yolks, sugar, and vanilla. Mix thoroughly.

Next, prepare the batter. In a large bowl, cream the butter and sugar. Add the eggs and beat well.

In another bowl, mix the flour and baking powder. Add this to the egg mixture alternately with the sour cream and the orange juice. Stir only until moistened.

Turn half the batter into the prepared baking dish. Spread the filling over the batter. (The filling will be thick.) Cover with the remaining batter and bake for 50 minutes or until puffed up and lightly browned.

Let the soufflé set for 10 minutes.

Meanwhile, make the fruit sauce. Heat the jam in a saucepan until melted. Stir in the blueberries and strawberries and heat until the mixture is heated through.

Cut the soufflé into squares and serve immediately, with the warm fruit sauce.

Yield: 8 servings; 2 cups of fruit sauce

Muffined Eggs with Cheese Sauce

12 eggs
6 tablespoons all-purpose flour
6 tablespoons plus ¼ cup butter or margarine
2½ cups half-and-half
2 cups grated sharp Cheddar cheese (8 ounces)
2 teaspoons powdered mustard
1 teaspoon Worcestershire sauce
Salt and pepper to taste
6 English muffins, halved
3 medium tomatoes, sliced

Preheat the oven to 350°F. Grease 12 non-stick muffin cups and drop one egg into each. Bake for 8 – 12 minutes or until set.

Heat the flour and 6 tablespoons of the butter in a heavy saucepan for 2 minutes. In another saucepan, heat the cream, taking care not to let it boil. Gradually stir the cream into the flour and butter mixture until it begins to thicken. Stir in the cheese, mustard, Worcestershire sauce, and salt and pepper.

Butter the English muffin halves using the remaining ¼ cup of butter and place one slice of tomato on each. Top with a baked egg, then the cheese sauce.

Serve immediately.

Yield: 12 servings

Cheese and Bacon Puffs

½ cup softened butter (¼ pound)
2 tablespoons mayonnaise
1 (5-ounce) jar cheese spread (see note)
6 slices bacon, cooked and crumbled
6 English muffins, halved

Blend the butter, mayonnaise, cheese spread, and bacon in a food processor.

Spread the mixture over the English muffin halves, then cut the halves in two.

Broil until puffy and light brown, or preheat the oven to 350°F and bake for 15 minutes.

Serve immediately, as an accompaniment to an egg dish.

Note: I recommend Kraft Old English brand cheese spread.

Yield: 8 servings (24 puffs)

Cheese Strata

This dish must be prepared the night before, then baked just before serving time.

8 slices white bread, cubed
2 cups grated sharp Cheddar cheese (8 ounces)
8 eggs
¼ cup butter, melted (⅛ pound)
2 cups milk
½ teaspoon powdered mustard

Grease a 6-cup soufflé dish.

Layer the bread and cheese in the prepared soufflé dish, ending with a layer of cheese.

Combine the eggs, melted butter, milk, and powdered mustard in a food processor and spread the mixture over the bread and cheese. Cover and refrigerate for at least 8 hours, or overnight.

Preheat the oven to 350°F and bake for 60 minutes or until puffed up and golden.

Cut into wedges and serve immediately.

Note: For variety, add cooked shrimp, ham, or bacon to the bread and cheese layers.

Yield:* 6 – 8 *servings

New England Cheddar Cheese Pie

9-inch Piecrust
1¼ cups all-purpose flour
½ teaspoon salt
½ cup vegetable shortening
3 tablespoons cold water

Filling
4 eggs
⅓ cup heavy whipping cream
4 cups grated Cheddar cheese (1 pound)
6 scallions, thinly sliced
Salt and pepper to taste
Tabasco sauce to taste
½ cup finely chopped walnuts

First, make the piecrust. Combine the flour with the salt. Cut in the shortening with a pastry blender or two knives until the mixture resembles coarse meal. Add the water and form into a ball, handling the dough as little as possible.

Flatten the dough slightly on a floured pastry cloth. Cover a rolling pin with a floured stockinette and roll the dough out 2 inches larger than the pie plate. Ease into the plate and flute the edges with your thumb and index finger.

Preheat the oven to 350°F.

To make the filling, whisk the eggs with the cream. Add the cheese, scallions, salt and pepper, and Tabasco sauce. Turn into the piecrust and top with the walnuts.

Bake for 25 minutes or until set. Cut into wedges and serve warm.

***Yield:** 8 servings*

Basil-Cheese Tart

8 ounces softened cream cheese
⅓ cup ricotta cheese
¼ cup softened butter (⅛ pound)
2 eggs
2 tablespoons all-purpose flour
3 tablespoons chopped fresh basil
½ teaspoon salt
¼ teaspoon pepper
1 (9-inch) piecrust, unbaked (see recipe on page 55)

Preheat the oven to 350°F.

Using an electric mixer, beat the cream cheese, ricotta cheese, and butter until light and fluffy. Add the eggs one at a time, beating well after each addition. Add the flour, basil, salt, and pepper. Beat until blended.

Turn into the piecrust and bake for 30 – 40 minutes or until set and lightly browned.

Cut into wedges and serve hot or at room temperature.

Yield: 8 servings

Fresh Corn Quiche

3 eggs
1 (¼-inch) slice of onion
1 tablespoon sugar
1 tablespoon all-purpose flour
1 teaspoon salt
3 tablespoons butter, melted
1⅓ cups half-and-half, scalded
2 cups uncooked fresh corn, or frozen, thawed
1 (9-inch) piecrust, unbaked (see recipe on page 55)

Preheat the oven to 375°F.

In a food processor, combine the eggs, onion, sugar, flour, and salt. Add the butter and cream and blend. Fold in the corn.

Turn the mixture into the piecrust and bake for 45 minutes or until slightly puffed up and lightly browned.

Cut into wedges and serve immediately.

Yield:* 6 – 8 *servings

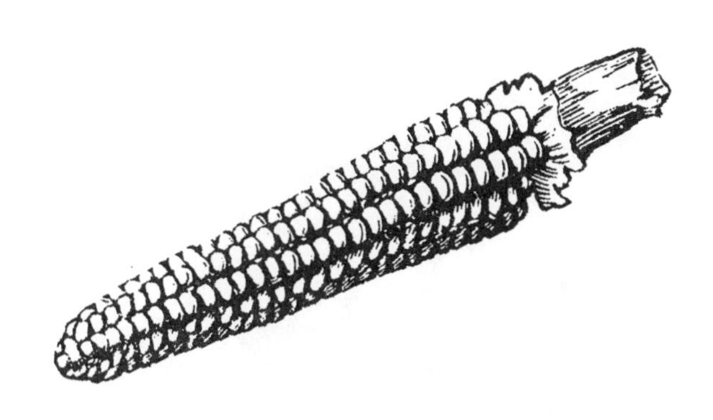

Potato Quiche

1 (1-pound, 4-ounce) package frozen shredded hash brown potatoes, thawed
⅓ cup margarine or butter, melted (⅙ pound)
1½ teaspoons dried beef bouillon granules
4 eggs, beaten
⅓ cup chopped onion (½ medium)
2 cups creamed cottage cheese
1 cup grated Monterey Jack cheese (4 ounces)

Preheat the oven to 400°F. Grease a 10-inch pie plate.

Combine the thawed potatoes, margarine, and bouillon. Spoon into the prepared pie plate and press onto the bottom and sides to form a crust. Bake for 25 minutes.

Meanwhile, combine the eggs, onion, cottage cheese, and Monterey Jack cheese. Turn into the baked potato crust. Reduce the oven temperature to 350°F and bake for another 30 – 35 minutes or until puffed up and golden.

Cut into wedges and serve warm.

Yield: 8 servings

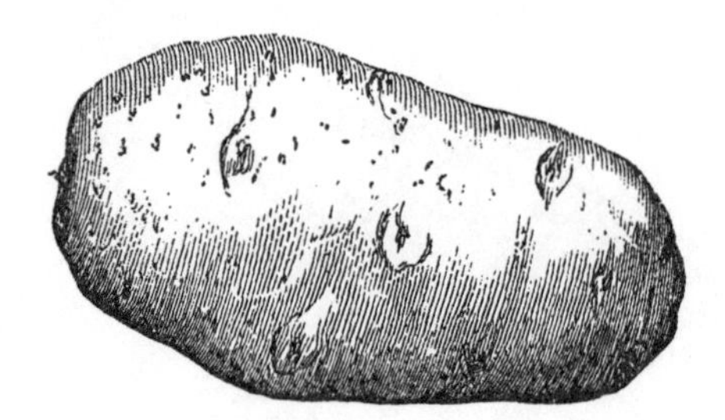

Vegetable Quiche with Potato Crust

2 large or 3 medium russet potatoes,
baked, cooled, and mashed (1½ cups) (see note)
2 tablespoons butter, melted
1 tablespoon all-purpose flour
½ cup chopped onion (1 small)
½ cup chopped red pepper (½ small)
½ cup grated sharp Cheddar cheese (2 ounces)
3 eggs, lightly beaten
½ cup milk
Salt and pepper to taste

Preheat the oven to 375°F. Lightly grease a 9-inch pie plate.

In a small bowl, combine the mashed potato, 1 tablespoon of the melted butter, and the flour. Transfer the mixture to the prepared pie plate and press evenly onto the bottom and sides. Bake for 10 minutes or until barely golden.

Heat the remaining tablespoon of butter in a small frying pan and sauté the onion and red pepper for 5 – 7 minutes or until tender. Arrange in the potato crust. Top with the grated cheese.

In a small bowl, beat the eggs with the milk. Season with salt and pepper and pour over the mixture in the crust.

Bake for 30 minutes or until set in the center. Cool slightly before cutting into wedges.

Serve warm.

Note: You can use commercially prepared mashed potatoes if this is more convenient.

Yield: 6 servings

Chicken-Pecan Quiche

2 cups finely chopped cooked chicken
1 cup grated Monterey Jack cheese (4 ounces)
¼ cup chopped scallions
1 tablespoon chopped fresh parsley
1 tablespoon all-purpose flour
1 (9-inch) piecrust, unbaked (see recipe on page 55)
3 eggs, beaten
1¼ cups half-and-half
½ teaspoon Dijon mustard
½ cup chopped pecans

Preheat the oven to 325°F.

Mix the chicken, cheese, scallions, parsley, and flour. Sprinkle into the piecrust.

Mix the eggs, cream, and mustard and pour this over the chicken mixture. Top with the pecans and bake for 60 minutes or until lightly browned.

Cut into wedges and serve warm.

Yield: 8 servings

Beef and Cheddar Cheese Quiche

½ pound lean ground beef
¼ cup chopped onion (½ small)
Dash of salt and pepper
3 eggs
½ cup milk
2 cups grated sharp Cheddar cheese (8 ounces)
½ cup mayonnaise
1 (9-inch) piecrust, unbaked (see recipe on page 55)

Preheat the oven to 350°F.

In a frying pan, brown the beef with the onion. Drain. Sprinkle with the salt and pepper.

Combine the eggs, milk, cheese, and mayonnaise and add to the beef mixture, mixing well. Turn into the piecrust and bake for 35 – 40 minutes or until slightly puffed up and browned.

Cut into wedges and serve warm.

Yield: 8 servings

Creamed Beef Casserole

½ cup butter (¼ pound)
4 tablespoons all-purpose flour
4 cups milk
½ pound chipped beef, cut into small pieces
4 slices bacon, cooked and crumbled
2 (3-ounce) cans sliced mushrooms, drained
Pepper to taste
16 eggs
1 cup half-and-half

Melt half the butter (4 tablespoons) in a medium saucepan. Add the flour and milk and heat slowly, stirring constantly, to make a medium white sauce. Mix in the beef, bacon, mushrooms, and pepper.

Lightly beat the eggs and cream.

Melt the remaining 4 tablespoons of butter in a large frying pan. Add the egg mixture and scramble.

Preheat the oven to 275°F. Grease a 13 x 9 x 2-inch glass baking dish.

Alternate layers of scrambled egg and beef sauce in the prepared baking dish. Cover with aluminum foil and bake for 60 minutes or until heated through.

Cut into squares and serve immediately.

Yield: 8 servings

Baked Pork Sausage for a Crowd

Preheat the oven to 350°F.

Allowing at least two per serving, drop link pork sausages into boiling water to cover. Simmer for 5 minutes and drain.

Arrange the sausages on a rack over a shallow pan. Brush with melted butter and bake for 30 minutes.

Note: Serve with French toast or scrambled eggs.

Yield: 1 serving (2 sausages)

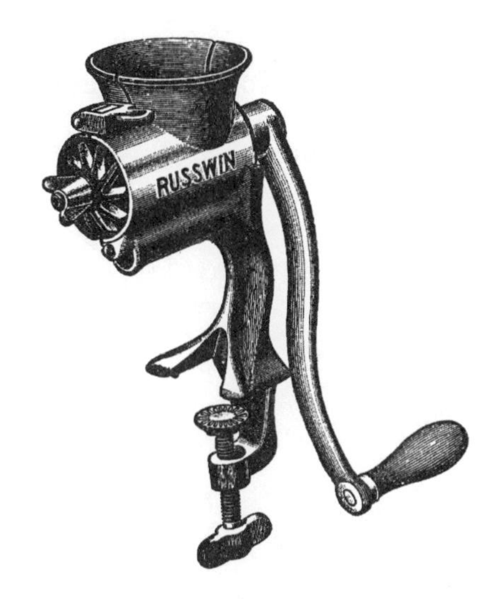

Ham-and-Apple Pie

¾ cup brown sugar
3 tablespoons all-purpose flour
½ teaspoon ground cinnamon
½ teaspoon ground mace
Dash of pepper
6 cups peeled and sliced tart apple (6 medium)
¼ – ½ pound cooked ham, cut into small pieces
Piecrust, unbaked (see recipe on page 55)
Cheddar, Gouda, or Monterey Jack cheese

Preheat the oven to 325°F. Grease a 13 x 9 x 2-inch glass baking dish.

Combine the sugar, flour, cinnamon, mace, and pepper.

Place 2 cups of the apple in the prepared baking dish. Layer half the ham over the apple. Sprinkle with half the sugar mixture. Layer with another 2 cups of the apple, the remaining ham, and the remaining sugar mixture. Top with the remaining apple.

Instead of rolling the pie dough to fit a pie plate, roll it out to 13 x 9 inches and use it to cover the apple in the dish. Seal the edges and bake for 60 minutes.

Cut into squares and serve hot, with the cheese.

Yield: 8 servings

Apple-Sausage Ring

2 pounds bulk sausage
2 eggs, lightly beaten
¼ cup minced onion (½ small)
½ cup milk
1½ cups seasoned herb stuffing
1 cup peeled chopped apple (1 medium)

Preheat the oven to 350°F. Grease a baking sheet.

Mix all the ingredients until thoroughly combined. Form the mixture into a ring on the prepared baking sheet and bake for 60 minutes or until browned.

Drain and cut into serving slices.

Serve hot.

Yield: 8 servings

Fruit Kugel

1 (1-pound) package wide egg noodles
2 cups milk
2 cups small-curd cottage cheese
2 cups sour cream
4 eggs, beaten
1 cup sugar
½ cup butter, melted (¼ pound)
1 (17¼-ounce) can crushed pineapple, drained
¾ cup finely chopped dried apricot (3 ounces)
Cornflake crumbs
Cinnamon sugar (see note)
Butter

Preheat the oven to 350°F. Grease a 15 x 10 x 2-inch glass baking dish.

Cook and drain the noodles.

Combine the milk, cottage cheese, sour cream, eggs, sugar, melted butter, pineapple, and apricot. Add the noodles and turn into the prepared baking dish. Top with the cornflakes and sprinkle with the cinnamon sugar.

Dot with unmelted butter and bake for 60 minutes or until a knife inserted in the center comes out clean. Cool for 15 minutes.

Cut into squares and serve warm.

Note: To make cinnamon sugar, combine 1 teaspoon of ground cinnamon and 2 tablespoons of sugar.

Yield: 10 – 12 servings

Blueberry Clafouti

2 tablespoons plus ⅓ cup granulated sugar
2 cups fresh blueberries (1 pint)
1¼ cups milk
½ cup all-purpose flour
2 eggs plus 2 egg yolks
1½ teaspoons vanilla
Pinch of salt
Confectioners' sugar

Preheat the oven to 400°F. Grease a 10-inch glass pie plate or ceramic quiche dish.

Sprinkle the prepared plate with the 2 tablespoons of granulated sugar. Arrange the blueberries over the bottom.

In a food processor, combine the milk, flour, eggs, egg yolks, vanilla, salt, and remaining ⅓ cup of granulated sugar. Blend until smooth. Pour the mixture over the blueberries.

Bake for 30 – 35 minutes or until puffed up and golden. Cool for 5 minutes.

Cut into wedges and serve warm, dusted with confectioners' sugar.

Yield: 6 – 8 servings

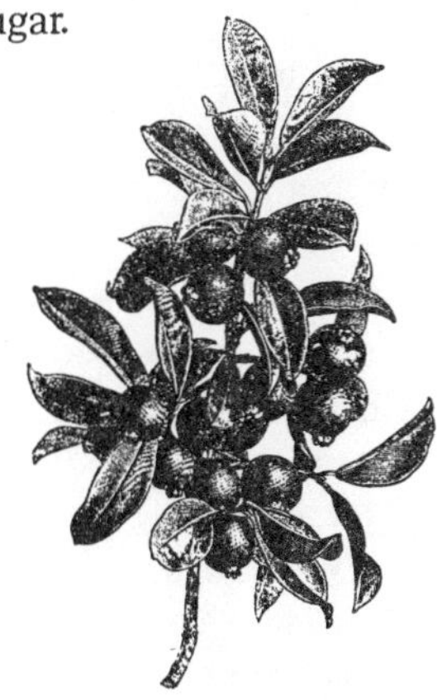

Apple Bread Pudding

This dish can be prepared the night before, then baked before serving time.

1 (1-pound) loaf firm raisin bread, sliced
¼ cup butter (⅛ pound)
3 cups peeled and sliced tart apple (3 medium)
2 tablespoons all-purpose flour
½ cup sugar
1 teaspoon ground cinnamon
4 eggs, lightly beaten
2½ cups milk
½ teaspoon salt
Maple syrup

If you plan to bake this dish immediately, preheat the oven to 350°F. Grease a 13 x 9 x 2-inch glass baking dish.

Remove the crusts from the bread and cut the slices into ¾-inch cubes.

In a medium frying pan, melt the butter. Add the apple and cook, stirring occasionally, for 5 minutes or until tender.

Combine the flour, 2 tablespoons of the sugar, and the cinnamon, and stir into the apple. Cook, stirring gently, for 1 minute or until thickened. Spoon into the prepared baking dish. Layer the bread cubes over the apple mixture.

In a medium bowl, mix the eggs, milk, salt, and remaining sugar. Pour over the bread cubes. Using a spoon, press down on the bread until it absorbs the egg mixture. Cover and refrigerate overnight, or bake immediately.

Bake for 50 – 70 minutes or until golden and a knife inserted in the center comes out clean. Cut into squares and serve warm, with the maple syrup.

Yield: 8 servings

Breads, Biscuits, & Muffins

Cheddar Cheese Date-Nut Bread

1 cup all-purpose flour
1 cup whole wheat flour
1 cup sugar
3 teaspoons baking powder
½ teaspoon salt
1 egg, beaten
¼ cup vegetable oil
1 cup milk
1 cup grated sharp Cheddar cheese (4 ounces)
½ cup chopped dates
½ cup chopped walnuts

Preheat the oven to 350°F. Grease a 9 x 5 x 3-inch loaf pan.

Mix the all-purpose flour, whole wheat flour, sugar, baking powder, and salt.

In a separate bowl, beat the egg, oil, and milk. Add to the flour mixture, stirring just until the dry ingredients are moistened. Fold in the cheese, dates, and walnuts.

Turn into the prepared loaf pan and bake for 45 minutes or until a wooden toothpick inserted in the center comes out clean. Turn out on a wire rack to cool.

Serve warm or at room temperature.

***Yield:** 1 loaf*

Walnut Bread

3½ cups all-purpose flour
3 cups whole wheat flour
1 cup chopped walnuts
⅓ cup sugar
4 teaspoons salt
2 packages fast-rising instant yeast (2 tablespoons)
¼ cup margarine (⅛ pound)
1½ cups water
¾ cup milk

Mix 2½ cups of the all-purpose flour, the whole wheat flour, walnuts, sugar, salt, and yeast.

In a saucepan, heat the margarine, water, and milk to 95° – 115°F. Mix this with the dry ingredients along with enough of the remaining 1 cup of all-purpose flour to make a soft dough.

Turn the dough onto a floured board and knead for 8 – 10 minutes. Cover with a tea towel and let rest for 10 minutes. Meanwhile, grease two 9 x 5 x 3-inch loaf pans.

Divide the dough and place it in the prepared loaf pans. Cover with a tea towel and let rise for 40 minutes or until doubled.

Preheat the oven to 400°F and bake for 30 minutes or until a wooden toothpick inserted in the center comes out clean. Turn out on a wire rack to cool.

Serve warm or at room temperature.

Yield: 2 loaves

Pecan Cornbread

1½ cups cornmeal
1 cup all-purpose flour
¼ cup sugar
1 tablespoon baking powder
1 teaspoon salt
1½ cups half-and-half
¾ cup butter, melted
2 eggs, lightly beaten
½ cup chopped pecans

Preheat the oven to 350°F. Grease a 13 x 9 x 2-inch baking pan.

Combine the cornmeal, flour, sugar, baking powder, and salt in a large bowl. Make a well in the center of the mixture.

Combine the cream with the butter, eggs, and pecans. Add this mixture to the dry ingredients, stirring just until they are moistened.

Turn the batter into the prepared baking pan and bake for 30 minutes or until golden.

Remove from the pan and and serve immediately or cool on a wire rack.

Cut into squares to serve.

***Yield:** 1 (13 x 9-inch) cornbread*

Blueberry-Nut Bread

3 cups all-purpose flour
2 teaspoons baking powder
1 teaspoon baking soda
½ teaspoon salt
⅔ cup vegetable oil
1⅓ cups sugar
4 eggs
½ cup milk
1½ teaspoons lemon juice
1 cup drained crushed pineapple (canned)
2 cups fresh blueberries (1 pint)
1 cup chopped pecans

Preheat the oven to 350°F. Grease and flour two 9 x 5 x 3-inch loaf pans.

Combine the flour, baking powder, baking soda, and salt.

In a large bowl, thoroughly mix the oil, sugar, eggs, milk, lemon juice, and pineapple. Blend in the flour mixture. Fold in the blueberries and pecans.

Spread the batter in the prepared pans and bake for 40 – 50 minutes or until a wooden toothpick inserted in the center comes out clean. Turn out on a wire rack to cool.

Serve warm or at room temperature.

Yield: 2 loaves

Banana-Chocolate Bread

This recipe, along with several others in the collection, comes from my friend Barbara Lambert, an excellent cook and a fellow chocoholic. I often include this sweet bread in my afternoon tea menus.

½ cup softened butter or margarine (¼ pound)
1 cup sugar
2 eggs
2 medium ripe bananas, mashed (1¼ cups)
2 cups all-purpose flour
1 teaspoon baking powder
½ teaspoon baking soda
½ teaspoon salt
¾ cup semisweet chocolate mini-morsels (4 – 5 ounces)
½ cup chopped walnuts

Preheat the oven to 350°F. Grease a 9 x 5 x 3-inch loaf pan.

Cream the butter. Using an electric mixer at medium speed, gradually add the sugar, beating well. Add the eggs one at a time, beating well after each addition. Stir in the banana.

Combine the flour with the baking powder, baking soda, and salt. Add to the butter mixture gradually, beating until blended. Stir in the chocolate and the walnuts.

Spoon the batter into the prepared pan and bake for 70 minutes or until a wooden toothpick inserted in the center comes out clean (cover with aluminum foil after 60 minutes to prevent over-browning).

Cool in the pan on a wire rack for 10 minutes, then turn out on the rack to finish cooling. Serve warm or at room temperature.

***Yield:** 1 loaf*

Apple Bread

4 cups all-purpose flour
2 teaspoons baking soda
2 teaspoons ground cinnamon
1 teaspoon salt
2 cups sugar
4 eggs, beaten
1 cup vegetable oil
¼ cup sour cream
2 teaspoons vanilla
2 cups peeled, chopped apple (2 medium)
1 cup chopped walnuts

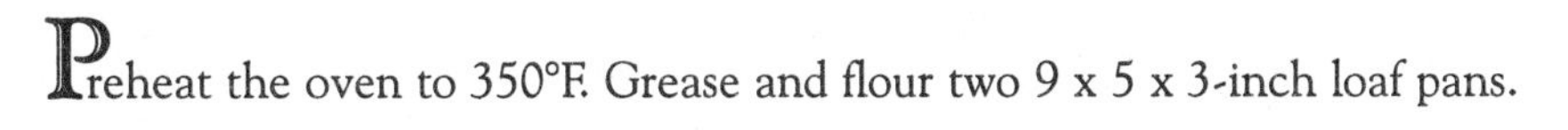

Preheat the oven to 350°F. Grease and flour two 9 x 5 x 3-inch loaf pans.

Combine the flour with the baking soda, cinnamon, and salt.

Combine the sugar, eggs, oil, sour cream, and vanilla. Beat well. Blend this mixture into the flour mixture. Fold in the apple and walnuts.

Turn into the prepared loaf pans and bake for 60 minutes or until a wooden toothpick inserted in the center comes out clean (check at 50 – 55 minutes). Turn out on a wire rack to cool.

Serve warm or at room temperature.

Yield: 2 loaves

Pumpkin-Apple Gingerbread

3½ cups all-purpose flour
3 teaspoons baking powder
½ teaspoon baking soda
2½ teaspoons ground ginger
½ teaspoon pumpkin pie spice
½ teaspoon salt
1 cup softened margarine or butter (½ pound)
1 cup granulated sugar
½ cup brown sugar
4 eggs
1 (15-ounce) can solid-packed pumpkin (1¾ cups)
1 large green apple, peeled, cored, and grated (1 cup)
½ cup molasses

Preheat the oven to 350°F. Grease and flour a 12-cup bundt pan.

In a medium bowl, mix the flour, baking powder, baking soda, ginger, pumpkin pie spice, and salt.

In a large bowl, using an electric mixer on medium speed, beat the margarine, granulated sugar, and brown sugar until creamy. Add the eggs two at a time, beating well after each addition. Beat in the pumpkin, apple, and molasses. Gradually beat in the flour mixture.

Turn into the prepared pan and bake for 60 minutes or until a wooden toothpick inserted in the center comes out clean. Cool in the pan on a wire rack for 15 minutes. Invert onto the rack and continue to cool.

Serve warm or at room temperature.

***Yield:** 14 – 16 servings*

Tangy Citrus Bread

2¼ cups all-purpose flour
¾ cup sugar
3 teaspoons baking powder
1 teaspoon salt
¾ cup chopped pecans
Zest of 2 lemons, grated
Zest of 2 limes, grated
1 egg
¼ cup lime juice
¾ cup lemon-lime soda
2 tablespoons vegetable oil

Glaze
½ cup confectioners' sugar
Juice of 1 large lemon

Preheat the oven to 350°F. Grease a 9 x 5 x 3-inch loaf pan.

Combine the flour, sugar, baking powder, and salt. Stir in the pecans, lemon zest, and lime zest.

Combine the egg, lime juice, lemon-lime soda, and oil. Add to the flour mixture, stirring just enough to moisten the dry ingredients. Turn the mixture into the prepared loaf pan and bake for 40 minutes or until lightly browned.

Cool in the pan for 10 minutes, then turn out on a wire rack to continue cooling.

Meanwhile, make the glaze. Mix the sugar with the lemon juice until smooth. Glaze while the bread is still warm.

Serve warm or at room temperature.

Yield: 1 loaf

Christmas Tree Bread

My assistant Jill Turner contributed this recipe — a holiday tradition from her childhood. Each year she bakes these little Christmas trees as a Yuletide treat for our guests.

1½ cups milk, warmed to 95° – 115°F
1 teaspoon plus ⅓ cup sugar
2 packages active dry yeast (2 tablespoons)
5 cups all-purpose flour
2 eggs
½ cup butter, at room temperature (¼ pound)
1 teaspoon salt
1¼ teaspoons ground cinnamon
½ cup raisins
1 cup chopped candied lemon and orange peel, or fruitcake mix
½ cup chopped candied red cherries
½ cup chopped candied green pineapple
Holiday baking decorations or chopped red and green candied fruit

GLAZE
½ cup confectioners' sugar
1 – 2 teaspoons milk
¼ teaspoon vanilla

In a large bowl, mix ½ cup of the warmed milk with the 1 teaspoon of sugar, the yeast, and ½ cup of the flour. Let sit for 10 – 15 minutes or until bubbly.

Add the remaining 1 cup of milk and the ⅓ cup of sugar to the milk mixture. Using an electric mixer, beat in the eggs. Add 1 cup of the flour. Stir in the butter, salt, cinnamon, raisins, and candied peel, cherries, and pineapple. Using a dough hook or by hand, mix in just enough of the remaining flour to make the dough hold together and pull away from the sides of the bowl; the dough will be soft, slightly sticky, and kneadable.

Turn the dough onto a lightly floured surface and knead for 3 – 4 minutes. Let the dough rest while you clean and grease the mixing bowl. Knead the dough for another 5 minutes or until smooth. Add just enough flour to keep it from sticking to the board.

Return the dough to the greased bowl, turning it once to ensure that the entire surface of the dough is greased. Cover with a tea towel and let rise in a warm place for 1½ – 2 hours or until doubled.

Meanwhile, grease two or three baking sheets.

Punch down the dough and divide it into four sections. Roll each section into a long rope an inch thick. Pinch off 1-inch pieces and roll them into balls.

On each prepared baking sheet, place the balls slightly apart in a pyramid shape to create a Christmas tree. Start with four balls, then three, then two, and finally one ball at the top. Center a slightly larger, elongated ball at the base to form the tree trunk. The balls should be closely spaced yet not touching — they will join together during the second rise. Cover and return the dough, on the baking sheets, to a warm place. Let rise for 45 – 60 minutes or until doubled.

Preheat the oven to 350°F and bake for 15 – 20 minutes. Cool on wire racks.

To make the glaze, mix the sugar, milk, and vanilla until smooth.

Before serving, drizzle each tree with the glaze and sprinkle with the holiday baking decorations or chopped red and green candied fruit.

Serve at room temperature.

Yield: 8 small Christmas trees

(You can make one large tree by shaping the dough into 2½-inch balls and using six balls at the base to form the trunk.)

Angel Biscuits with Rosy Apple Butter

Rosy Apple Butter

4 pounds Granny Smith apples, peeled, cored, and thinly sliced (8 medium)
1 cup fresh cranberries (4 ounces)
1½ cups sweet apple cider
3 (3 x 1-inch) strips lemon peel
3 tablespoons lemon juice
1½ cups sugar

Angel Biscuits

1 package active dry yeast (1 tablespoon)
2 tablespoons warm water (95° – 115°F)
5 cups all-purpose flour
2 tablespoons sugar
3 teaspoons baking powder
1 teaspoon baking soda
1½ teaspoons salt
1 cup vegetable shortening
2 cups buttermilk
Melted butter

To make the apple butter, bring the apple, cranberries, cider, lemon peel, and lemon juice to a boil over high heat in a large Dutch oven. Reduce heat and, stirring occasionally, simmer, uncovered, for 15 minutes or until the apple is soft. Remove the lemon peel. Stir in the sugar. Partially cover and, stirring occasionally, cook over medium heat for 60 minutes or until very thick.

Spoon the apple butter into a food processor, in batches. Blend until smooth. Cool.

To make the angel biscuits, preheat the oven to 400°F.

Dissolve the yeast in the water and leave for 5 – 10 minutes or until bubbly.

Combine the flour, sugar, baking powder, baking soda, and salt in a large bowl. Cut in the shortening with a pastry blender or two knives. Add the buttermilk, then the yeast mixture. Stir until the dry ingredients are thoroughly moistened.

Turn the dough onto a floured board and knead for 1 – 2 minutes. Roll out to a thickness of half an inch and cut into 2½-inch rounds.

Brush with the melted butter and bake on an ungreased baking sheet for 12 – 15 minutes or until lightly browned. Cool on a wire rack.

Serve warm or at room temperature, with the apple butter.

Note: Leftover apple butter can be refrigerated, in a tightly sealed container, for up to two weeks. It can also be frozen.

Yield: 30 biscuits; 5 cups of apple butter

Applesauce Cheese Biscuits

2 cups all-purpose flour
2 teaspoons baking powder
¼ teaspoon baking soda
1 teaspoon salt
¼ cup vegetable shortening
¾ cup applesauce
¾ cup grated sharp Cheddar cheese (3 ounces)

Preheat the oven to 400°F.

Combine the flour with the baking powder, baking soda, and salt. Cut in the shortening with a pastry blender or two knives. Add the applesauce and cheese and mix.

Roll out the dough to a thickness of half an inch and cut into 2-inch rounds. Place on an ungreased baking sheet and bake for 8 – 10 minutes or until lightly browned. Turn out on a wire rack to cool.

Serve warm or at room temperature.

Yield: 24 biscuits

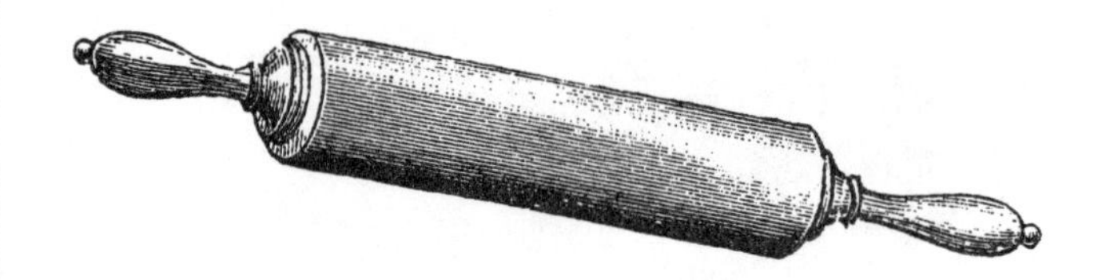

Fruit Scones

2 cups all-purpose flour
4 teaspoons baking powder
2 tablespoons sugar
1 teaspoon salt
7 tablespoons vegetable shortening
1 teaspoon grated orange zest
2 eggs, well beaten
½ cup orange juice
¼ cup chopped dates, chopped dried apricots, or raisins

Preheat the oven to 400°F.

Combine the flour with the baking powder, sugar, and salt. Cut in the shortening with a pastry blender or two knives. Add the orange zest and mix.

Combine the eggs and the orange juice. Add to the flour mixture and work into a soft dough. Fold in the dates.

Knead lightly and roll out to a thickness of about three quarters of an inch. Cut with a 2½-inch biscuit cutter.

Place on an ungreased baking sheet and bake for 12 – 15 minutes or until lightly browned. Cool on a wire rack.

Serve warm or at room temperature.

Yield: 24 scones

Cranberry-Walnut Scones

2 cups all-purpose flour
2 tablespoons plus 2 teaspoons sugar
2 teaspoons baking powder
½ teaspoon baking soda
½ teaspoon ground nutmeg
½ teaspoon salt
½ cup butter or margarine (¼ pound)
½ cup sweetened dried cranberries (3½ ounces)
½ cup chopped walnuts
¾ cup buttermilk
1 egg, separated

Preheat the oven to 375°F. Lightly grease a baking sheet or line it with parchment paper.

In a large bowl, mix the flour, the 2 tablespoons of sugar, baking powder, baking soda, nutmeg, and salt. Using a pastry blender or two knives, cut in the butter until the mixture is crumbly. Add the cranberries and walnuts and mix well.

In a small bowl, blend the buttermilk and egg yolk. Add to the flour mixture and stir just until the dry ingredients are moistened.

Turn the dough onto a lightly floured surface and knead lightly 12 times. Divide the dough in half and place on the prepared baking sheet. Pat each half into a 6-inch circle and cut into 6 wedges. Do not separate.

In a small bowl, beat the egg white slightly. Use this to brush the top of the scones. Sprinkle the scones with the remaining 2 teaspoons of sugar and bake for 15 – 20 minutes or until golden brown. Cool for 10 minutes on a wire rack.

Serve warm or at room temperature.

***Yield:** 12 scones*

Peachy Oat Muffins

1 (16-ounce) can peach halves in juice or extra light syrup
1 egg, beaten
¼ cup vegetable oil
1 teaspoon vanilla
½ teaspoon grated orange zest
¼ teaspoon almond extract
1 cup all-purpose flour
1 cup large-flake rolled oats
¾ cup brown sugar
2 teaspoons baking powder
1 teaspoon ground cinnamon
½ cup raisins

Preheat the oven to 400°F. Grease 12 muffin cups.

Drain the peaches, reserving the liquid for other uses (see note). Chop two of the peach halves and set aside. Purée the remaining peach halves to measure 1 cup. Combine the peach purée with the egg, oil, vanilla, orange zest, and almond extract.

In a large bowl, combine the flour, rolled oats, sugar, baking powder, and cinnamon. Mix well. Mix the peach purée mixture into the dry ingredients just until the dry ingredients are moistened. Fold in the chopped peaches and the raisins.

Scoop the batter into the prepared muffin cups. Bake for 20 minutes or until a wooden toothpick inserted in the center comes out clean. Turn out on a wire rack to cool.

Serve warm or at room temperature.

Note: You can use the reserved peach juice to flavor plain yogurt, cottage cheese, or orange or grapefruit slices.

Yield: 12 muffins

Light-as-a-Feather Lemon Muffins

1 cup butter (½ pound)
1 cup sugar
4 eggs, separated
2 cups all-purpose flour
2 teaspoons baking powder
½ teaspoon baking soda
1 teaspoon salt
½ cup lemon juice
2 teaspoons grated lemon zest

Preheat the oven to 375°F. Grease 12 muffin cups.

Cream the butter and sugar until smooth. Beat the egg yolks and add to the creamed mixture, beating until light and frothy.

Combine the flour, baking powder, baking soda, and salt. Add the flour mixture and the lemon juice alternately to the butter mixture, mixing after each addition. Beat the egg whites until stiff, then fold in, along with the lemon zest.

Fill the prepared muffin cups three quarters full and bake for 20 – 25 minutes or until a wooden toothpick inserted in the center comes out clean. Turn out on a wire rack to cool.

Serve warm or at room temperature.

Yield:* *12 muffins

Very Berry Streusel Muffins

2 cups all-purpose flour
½ cup sugar
2 teaspoons baking powder
½ teaspoon baking soda
½ teaspoon salt
1 (8-ounce) container lemon yogurt
½ cup vegetable oil
1 teaspoon grated lemon zest
2 eggs
½ cup fresh raspberries (scant ¼ pint)
½ cup fresh blueberries (¼ pint)

TOPPING
⅓ cup sugar
¼ cup all-purpose flour
2 tablespoons butter

Preheat the oven to 400°F. Grease 12 muffin cups.

In a large bowl, combine the flour, sugar, baking powder, baking soda, and salt. Mix well.

In a small bowl, combine the yogurt, oil, lemon zest, and eggs. Mix well. Add to the flour mixture, stirring just until the dry ingredients are moistened. Gently stir in the raspberries and blueberries. Fill the prepared muffin cups.

Next, make the topping. In a small bowl, combine the sugar and flour. Using a pastry blender or two knives, cut in the butter until the mixture is crumbly.

Sprinkle the topping over the muffins and bake for 18 – 20 minutes or until a wooden toothpick inserted in the center comes out clean. Turn out on a wire rack to cool.

Serve warm or at room temperature.

***Yield:** 12 muffins*

Poppy Seed-Orange Muffins

1⅓ cups all-purpose flour
1 cup sugar
½ cup sour cream
⅓ cup softened butter (⅙ pound)
1 egg
2 tablespoons grated orange zest
2 tablespoons orange juice
1 tablespoon poppy seed
½ teaspoon salt
½ teaspoon baking soda

Preheat the oven to 400°F. Grease 12 muffin cups.

In a large bowl, using an electric mixer at low speed, beat all the ingredients for 1 minute or until the dry ingredients are just moistened. Scrape the bowl often.

Scoop the batter into the prepared muffin cups and bake for 15 – 20 minutes or until lightly browned. Turn out on a wire rack to cool.

Serve warm or a room temperature.

Yield:* *12 muffins

Pineapple Muffins

1 cup chopped pecans
2 cups all-purpose flour
1 teaspoon baking soda
1 teaspoon salt
3 ounces softened cream cheese (6 tablespoons)
1 cup sugar
2 teaspoons vanilla
1 egg, beaten
½ cup sour cream
1 (20-ounce) can crushed pineapple, drained

Preheat the oven to 375°F. Grease well 12 muffin cups and sprinkle in the pecans.

Combine the flour with the baking soda and salt.

In a large bowl, beat the cream cheese, sugar, and vanilla. Add the beaten egg and mix.

Mix the flour mixture into the cream cheese mixture alternately with the sour cream. Fold in the pineapple.

Scoop the batter into the prepared muffin cups and bake for 20 – 25 minutes or until lightly browned. Turn out on a wire rack to cool.

Serve warm or at room temperature.

Yield: 12 muffins

Gingerbread Muffins

2 cups all-purpose flour
1½ teaspoons baking powder
½ teaspoon baking soda
1½ teaspoons ground ginger
1 teaspoon ground cinnamon
½ teaspoon ground nutmeg
¼ teaspoon ground cloves
¼ teaspoon salt
1 egg, beaten
¾ cup milk
¼ cup molasses
¼ cup maple syrup
2 tablespoons sugar
½ cup chopped dates
¼ cup butter, melted (⅛ pound)

Preheat the oven to 350°F. Grease 12 muffin cups.

In a large bowl, stir the flour, baking powder, baking soda, ginger, cinnamon, nutmeg, cloves, and salt until thoroughly mixed.

To the beaten egg, add the milk, molasses, maple syrup, sugar, dates, and melted butter, mixing well. Pour this over the flour mixture and stir just until the dry ingredients are well mixed in.

Scoop the batter into the prepared muffin cups and bake for 20 minutes or until a wooden toothpick inserted in the center comes out clean. Turn out on a wire rack to cool.

Serve warm or at room temperature.

Yield: 12 muffins

Cheese Muffins

2 cups all-purpose flour
3 teaspoons baking powder
1 tablespoon sugar
½ teaspoon salt
1 egg
1 cup milk
3 tablespoons softened butter
1½ cups grated sharp Cheddar cheese (6 ounces)

Preheat the oven to 350°F. Grease 18 muffin cups (see note).

Mix the flour, baking powder, sugar, and salt in a medium bowl.

Blend the egg, milk, and butter in a food processor until smooth. Stir in the cheese. Mix the blended mixture into the flour mixture until the dry ingredients are just moistened.

Scoop the batter into the prepared muffin cups and bake for 25 minutes or until lightly browned. Turn out on a wire rack to cool.

Serve warm.

Note: Put a few tablespoons of water in any unused muffin cups to protect the pan and keep the rest of the muffins moist.

Yield: 18 muffins

Feta Cheese Corn Muffins

1 cup cornmeal
⅔ cup all-purpose flour
1 teaspoon baking powder
½ teaspoon baking soda
½ teaspoon salt
1 tablespoon finely chopped fresh basil
1 cup crumbled feta cheese (4 ounces)
1 cup milk
1 egg
¼ cup butter, melted (⅛ pound)

Preheat the oven to 425°F. Grease 12 muffin cups.

In a large bowl, whisk the cornmeal, flour, baking powder, baking soda, and salt. Add the basil and cheese and toss well.

In a small bowl, whisk the milk, egg, and melted butter. Add to the cornmeal mixture, stirring just until the batter is combined (do not overmix).

Scoop the batter into the prepared muffin cups and bake for 18 – 20 minutes or until golden and springy to the touch. Turn out on a wire rack to cool.

Serve warm or at room temperature.

Yield: 12 muffins

Blueberry Corn Muffins

1½ cups all-purpose flour
½ cup whole wheat flour
½ cup cornmeal
¾ cup sugar
2½ teaspoons baking powder
½ teaspoon baking soda
½ teaspoon salt
½ cup buttermilk
½ cup orange juice
¼ cup margarine or butter, melted (⅛ pound)
1 egg, beaten
1 tablespoon grated orange zest
2 cups fresh blueberries (1 pint)

Preheat the oven to 400°F. Grease 12 muffin cups.

In a large bowl, combine the all-purpose flour, whole wheat flour, cornmeal, sugar, baking powder, baking soda, and salt.

In a small bowl, combine the buttermilk, orange juice, margarine, egg, and orange zest. Add to the flour mixture and mix just until the dry ingredients are moistened. Fold in the blueberries.

Scoop the batter into the prepared muffin cups and bake for 20 – 25 minutes or until a wooden toothpick inserted in the center comes out clean. Turn out on a wire rack to cool.

Serve warm or at room temperature.

Yield: 12 muffins

Easy Miniature Corn Muffins

3 eggs, beaten
½ cup vegetable oil
1 (8¼-ounce) can creamed corn
1 cup sour cream
1 cup self-rising flour (see note)
½ cup bacon bits (2 ounces)
1 tablespoon minced dried onion
½ cup grated sharp Cheddar cheese (2 ounces)

Preheat the oven to 350°F. Grease well 24 miniature muffin cups.

Mix the eggs, vegetable oil, corn, and sour cream.

Combine the flour with the bacon and onion. Add this to the egg mixture, stirring only until blended.

Scoop the batter into the prepared muffin cups. Sprinkle a few shreds of cheese over each muffin and bake for 25 minutes or until lightly browned. Turn out on a wire rack to cool.

Serve warm.

Note: Self-rising flour is an all-purpose flour to which baking powder and salt have already been added.

Yield:* 24 *miniature muffins

Coffee Cakes

Almond Coffee Cake

FILLING
3½ ounces almond paste, cut up
½ cup confectioners' sugar
¼ cup margarine or butter (⅛ pound)
½ cup sliced almonds

CAKE
¾ cup softened margarine or butter
1½ cups sugar
3 eggs
1½ teaspoons vanilla
3 cups all-purpose flour
1½ teaspoons baking powder
1½ teaspoons baking soda
¾ teaspoon salt
1½ cups sour cream

GLAZE
½ cup confectioners' sugar
¼ teaspoon vanilla
1 – 2 teaspoons milk

Preheat the oven to 325°F. Grease a 10-inch tube pan.

First, prepare the filling. Heat the almond paste, sugar, and margarine over medium heat, stirring constantly, until smooth. Stir in the almonds.

Next, make the cake. In a large bowl, with an electric mixer set on medium speed, beat the margarine, sugar, eggs, and vanilla for 2 minutes, scraping the bowl occasionally.

In a separate bowl, mix the flour, baking powder, baking soda, and salt. With the mixer set on low speed, beat the flour mixture alternately with the sour cream into the margarine mixture.

Turn one third of the batter into the prepared pan. Sprinkle with one third of the filling. Repeat twice.

Bake for 45 minutes or until a wooden toothpick inserted in the center comes out clean. Cool on a wire rack for 20 minutes, while making the glaze.

To make the glaze, combine the sugar and vanilla. Stir in enough milk for desired drizzling consistency.

Turn the cake out on a plate and drizzle with the glaze. Cut into slices and serve warm or at room temperature.

Yield: 14 – 16 servings

Overnight Apple Cake

This recipe and several others in this collection were given to me by my sister Beverley Blackwell, who joined me in cooking up lots of mischief in our youth. Note that this cake should not be served until the day after it is made.

2 cups sugar
1½ cups vegetable oil
3 eggs
2 teaspoons vanilla
3 cups all-purpose flour
1 teaspoon baking soda
1 teaspoon salt
3 cups peeled, chopped apple (3 medium)
1 cup raisins
1 cup chopped pecans

GLAZE
½ cup butter (¼ pound)
1 cup sugar
½ cup buttermilk
1 tablespoon vanilla
½ teaspoon baking soda

Preheat the oven to 350°F. Grease and flour a 10-inch tube pan.

In a large bowl, blend the sugar and oil. Add the eggs and vanilla and mix.

Combine 2½ cups of the flour with the baking soda and salt. Stir into the sugar mixture.

Combine the apple, raisins, pecans, and remaining ½ cup of flour. Add this to the batter and mix well.

Turn the batter into the prepared pan and bake for 90 minutes or until a wooden toothpick inserted in the center comes out clean (do this in several spots in case you hit some apple).

To make the glaze, place the butter, sugar, buttermilk, vanilla, and baking soda in a saucepan and boil for 5 minutes, stirring constantly. Spoon over the hot cake.

Leave the cake in the pan. Cool on a wire rack, then refrigerate for at least 8 hours, or overnight, before serving.

Turn out onto a cake plate and cut into slices. Serve cool or at room temperature.

Yield: 14 – 16 servings

Jewish Apple Cake

3 cups all-purpose flour
3 teaspoons baking powder
1 teaspoon salt
4 eggs
2 cups sugar
1 cup vegetable oil
½ cup orange juice
2½ teaspoons vanilla
2 large apples, peeled, cored, and sliced (2 cups)
Cinnamon sugar (see note)

Preheat the oven to 350°F. Grease and flour a 10-inch tube pan.

Beat the flour, baking powder, salt, eggs, sugar, oil, orange juice, and vanilla for 2 minutes.

Turn half the batter into the prepared pan. Add a layer of apple. Sprinkle with half the cinnamon sugar. Add the rest of the batter and top with the remaining apple, then the remaining cinnamon sugar.

Bake for 60 minutes or until lightly browned. Cool on a wire rack.

Turn out onto a cake plate and slice. Serve warm or at room temperature.

Note: To make cinnamon sugar, mix 1 teaspoon of ground cinnamon and 2 tablespoons of sugar.

Yield:* *10 – 12 servings

Applesauce Cake

4 teaspoons baking soda
2½ cups hot applesauce
1 cup butter (½ pound)
2 cups brown sugar
4 cups all-purpose flour
3 cups raisins
1 teaspoon ground nutmeg
1 teaspoon ground cinnamon
1 teaspoon ground allspice
3½ cups chopped walnuts (1 pound)

Preheat the oven to 275°F. Grease and flour a 10-inch tube pan.

Stir the baking soda into the hot applesauce and let the mixture cool while you mix the other ingredients.

In a large bowl, cream the butter and sugar. Mix in the flour, raisins, nutmeg, cinnamon, allspice, and walnuts. Stir in the applesauce.

Turn into the prepared pan and bake for 2 hours or until a wooden toothpick inserted in the center comes out clean. Cool on a wire rack.

Turn out onto a cake plate. Cut into slices and serve warm or at room temperature.

Yield: 14 – 16 servings

Apricot Coffee Cake

¾ cup softened butter
¾ cup sugar
2 cups all-purpose flour
¾ teaspoon baking powder
¾ teaspoon baking soda
½ teaspoon salt
½ cup low-fat plain yogurt
½ cup ricotta cheese
½ cup milk
2 large eggs
1 teaspoon vanilla
¾ cup chopped dried apricot

Topping
½ cup sugar
⅓ cup all-purpose flour
¼ cup butter, melted (⅛ pound)
½ cup chopped pecans

Preheat the oven to 350°F. Grease a 13 x 9 x 2-inch baking pan.

In a large bowl, cream the butter and sugar using an electric mixer.

In a medium bowl, combine the flour, baking powder, baking soda, and salt.

In another bowl, combine the yogurt, cheese, milk, eggs, and vanilla.

Add the flour mixture alternately with the yogurt mixture to the butter mixture, beating well after each addition. Stir in the apricot. Turn the batter into the prepared pan.

To make the topping, combine the sugar, flour, and melted butter until the mixture resembles coarse meal. Stir in the pecans.

Sprinkle the topping over the batter and bake for 45 minutes or until a wooden toothpick inserted in the center comes out clean. Cool on a wire rack.

Cut into squares and serve warm or at room temperature.

Yield: 10 – 12 servings

Banana Crunch Coffee Cake

CAKE

⅔ cup butter (⅓ pound)
1⅔ cups sugar
3 eggs
1¼ cups mashed banana (2 medium)
2¼ cups all-purpose flour
1¼ teaspoons baking powder
1¼ teaspoons baking soda
1 teaspoon salt
⅔ cup buttermilk

TOPPING

¾ cup brown sugar
½ cup chopped pecans
1¼ cups sweetened flaked coconut
⅓ cup margarine or butter (⅙ pound)
2 tablespoons milk

Preheat the oven to 350°F. Grease a 13 x 9 x 2-inch baking pan.

In a large mixing bowl, cream the butter and sugar. Add the eggs one at a time, beating after each addition. Stir in the banana.

Combine the flour, baking powder, baking soda, and salt. Add this to the butter mixture alternately with the buttermilk, mixing after each addition. Turn into the prepared pan and bake for 45 minutes or until a wooden toothpick inserted in the center comes out clean.

To make the topping, combine all the ingredients. Spread while the cake is still warm. Broil for a few minutes or until golden and bubbly. Cool on a wire rack.

Cut into squares and serve warm or at room temperature.

Note: This cake freezes well. Thaw and broil just before serving.

***Yield:** 10 – 12 servings*

Blueberry Breakfast Cake

¼ cup softened butter (⅛ pound)
¾ cup sugar
1 egg
2 cups all-purpose flour
2 teaspoons baking powder
½ teaspoon salt
½ cup milk
2 cups fresh blueberries (1 pint)

Topping
½ cup sugar
⅓ cup all-purpose flour
½ teaspoon ground cinnamon
¼ cup softened butter (⅛ pound)

Preheat the oven to 350°F. Grease a 13 x 9 x 2-inch baking pan.

Cream the butter, sugar, and egg.

Combine the flour with the baking powder and salt and add to the butter mixture alternately with the milk, mixing after each addition. Fold in the blueberries and turn into the prepared pan.

To prepare the topping, mix the sugar, flour, cinnamon, and butter. Spread this over the batter in the pan.

Bake for 40 – 45 minutes or until a wooden toothpick inserted in the center comes out clean. Cool on a wire rack.

Cut into squares and serve warm or at room temperature.

Yield: 10 – 12 servings

Winter Blueberry Cake

½ cup butter or margarine (¼ pound)
1 cup sugar
3 eggs
2½ cups all-purpose flour, plus a small amount to coat fruit
3 teaspoons baking powder
½ teaspoon salt
1 teaspoon grated orange zest
½ cup milk
2 cups frozen blueberries, partially thawed (16 ounces)
1 cup peeled, diced pear or apple (1 medium)
½ cup diced dried apricot

Preheat the oven to 350°F. Grease a 10-inch tube pan.

Cream the butter and sugar until light and fluffy. Beat in the eggs one at a time.

Combine the flour, baking powder, salt, and orange zest. Mix well. Add the flour mixture alternately with the milk to the butter mixture.

Combine the blueberries, pear, and apricot and toss with a small amount of flour.

Spread half the batter in the prepared pan. Spoon the blueberry mixture over the batter. Top with the remaining batter and bake for 60 minutes or until golden brown and a wooden toothpick inserted in the center comes out clean. Cool on a wire rack for 10 minutes, then carefully invert onto a plate.

Cut into slices and serve warm.

Yield: 10 – 12 servings

Lemon-Blueberry Cake

This recipe was given to me by Christy Igoe, who owns the Sea Holly Inn, a lovely bed & breakfast in Cape May.

3 cups all-purpose flour
½ teaspoon baking soda
½ teaspoon salt
1 cup margarine or butter (½ pound)
2 teaspoons lemon extract
3 cups sugar
6 eggs
1 cup sour cream
1½ cups fresh blueberries (¾ pint)

Preheat the oven to 350°F. Grease and flour a 10-inch tube pan.

In a medium bowl, combine the flour, baking soda, and salt.

In a large bowl, cream the margarine with an electric mixer. Stir in the lemon extract. Add the sugar gradually and beat for 2 minutes. Add the eggs two at a time, beating thoroughly after each addition and for 2 – 3 minutes after the last addition. On the lowest speed, add half the flour mixture, beating only until blended. Add the sour cream, then the remaining flour mixture. Mix until smooth. Stir in the blueberries.

Turn into the prepared pan and bake for 60 – 80 minutes or until a wooden toothpick inserted in the center comes out clean. Cool on a wire rack for 20 minutes, then turn out onto a cake plate.

Cut into slices and serve warm or at room temperature.

Yield:* 14 – 16 *servings

Cherry Coffee Cake

3 eggs
1 cup sugar
⅓ cup orange juice
¾ cup vegetable oil
3 cups all-purpose flour
3½ teaspoons baking powder
¼ teaspoon salt
1 teaspoon vanilla
1 (11-ounce) can cherry pie filling
Cinnamon sugar (see note)

Preheat the oven to 350°F. Grease a 13 x 9 x 2-inch baking pan.

Beat the eggs. Add the sugar, orange juice, and oil, mixing well.

Combine the flour, baking powder, and salt. Fold this into the egg mixture. Add the vanilla and mix.

Spread half the batter in the prepared pan. Top with the pie filling. Cover with the rest of the batter and sprinkle with the cinnamon sugar. Bake for 45 minutes or until lightly browned. Cool on a wire rack.

Cut into squares and serve warm or at room temperature.

Note: To make cinnamon sugar, mix 1 teaspoon of ground cinnamon and 2 tablespoons of sugar.

Yield: 10 – 12 servings

Cranberry-Orange Coffee Cake

1½ cups softened butter (¾ pound)
2¾ cups sugar
1 teaspoon vanilla
1 teaspoon grated orange zest
6 eggs
3 cups all-purpose flour
1 teaspoon baking powder
½ teaspoon salt
1 cup sour cream
1½ cups chopped fresh cranberries (8 ounces)

Preheat the oven to 350°F. Grease and flour a 10-inch tube pan.

In a large bowl, beat the butter and sugar until light and fluffy. Stir in the vanilla and orange zest. Add the eggs one at a time, beating well after each addition.

In a medium bowl, combine the flour, baking powder, and salt. Add this to the butter mixture alternately with the sour cream, mixing after each addition. Stir in the cranberries.

Turn into the prepared pan and bake for 60 – 70 minutes or until a wooden toothpick inserted in the center comes out clean. Cool on a wire rack, then turn out onto a cake plate.

Cut into slices and serve warm or at room temperature.

Yield: 14 – 16 servings

Date-Nut Coffee Cake

1 cup chopped dates
1 cup sugar
7 tablespoons butter
2 teaspoons ground cinnamon
1 cup water
1 teaspoon baking soda
3 tablespoons boiling water
¾ cup chopped walnuts
2 cups all-purpose flour
1 teaspoon salt
1 teaspoon baking powder

GLAZE
1 cup confectioners' sugar
2 tablespoons milk
1 tablespoon butter, melted
1 teaspoon vanilla

Preheat the oven to 375°F. Grease a 13 x 9 x 2-inch baking pan.

Put the dates, sugar, butter, cinnamon, and the cup of water in a large saucepan. Simmer, stirring frequently, for 5 minutes. Dissolve the baking soda in the 3 tablespoons of boiling water. Stir this into the date mixture. Add the walnuts and stir well. Cool.

Combine the flour, salt, and baking powder. Add to the date mixture, beating well.

Spread the batter evenly in the prepared pan and bake for 20 minutes or until a wooden toothpick inserted in the center comes out clean. Cool on a wire rack.

To make the glaze, combine the sugar, milk, melted butter, and vanilla. Stir until smooth. Spread while the cake is still warm.

Cut into squares and serve warm or at room temperature.

Yield:* *10 – 12 servings

Mango Upside-Down Coffee Cake

2 tablespoons lemon juice
2 cups chopped ripe mango (2 medium)
2 tablespoons butter
⅓ cup brown sugar
¼ cup vegetable shortening
¾ cup granulated sugar
1 egg
1¼ cups all-purpose flour
1 teaspoon baking powder
¼ teaspoon salt
½ cup milk

Preheat the oven to 350°F.

Pour the lemon juice over the chopped mango.

Melt the butter in an 8-inch-square baking pan. Sprinkle with the brown sugar. Arrange the mango over the brown sugar.

In a large bowl, cream the shortening with the granulated sugar. Beat in the egg.

Combine the flour, baking powder, and salt. Add this to the shortening mixture alternately with the milk, mixing after each addition.

Spread the batter over the mango and bake for 45 – 55 minutes or until golden. Cool on a wire rack, then invert onto a cake plate.

Cut into squares and serve warm.

***Yield:** 6 – 8 servings*

Orange Kuchen

½ cup butter (¼ pound)
½ cup sugar
1 egg, beaten
Zest of 1 orange, grated
2 cups all-purpose flour
3 teaspoons baking powder
¼ teaspoon salt
¾ cup orange juice

TOPPING

½ cup brown sugar
1 teaspoon ground cinnamon
1 teaspoon ground nutmeg
1 tablespoon all-purpose flour
½ cup chopped walnuts
2 tablespoons butter

Preheat the oven to 350°F. Grease a 13 x 9 x 2-inch baking pan.

Beat the butter and sugar until light and fluffy. Add the egg and orange zest and beat well.

Combine the flour, baking powder, and salt. Add this to the butter mixture alternately with the orange juice, mixing after each addition. Turn the batter into the prepared baking pan.

To make the topping, combine the sugar, cinnamon, nutmeg, flour, and walnuts. Cut in the butter with a pastry blender or two knives until the mixture is crumbly.

Sprinkle the topping over the batter and bake for 25 – 30 minutes or until a wooden toothpick inserted in the center comes out clean. Cool on a wire rack.

Cut into squares and serve warm or at room temperature.

***Yield:** 10 – 12 servings*

Pineapple-Walnut Coffee Cake

½ cup butter (¼ pound)
1 cup brown sugar
2 eggs
1 teaspoon baking soda
1 cup sour cream
2 cups all-purpose flour
1 teaspoon baking powder
¼ teaspoon salt
1 teaspoon vanilla
1¼ cups drained crushed pineapple (canned)

Topping
¼ cup granulated sugar
⅓ cup brown sugar
½ cup chopped walnuts
¼ teaspoon ground cinnamon
¼ teaspoon ground nutmeg

Preheat the oven to 350°F. Grease a 13 x 9 x 2-inch baking pan.

Cream the butter and sugar. Add the eggs and beat well. Mix the baking soda into the sour cream. Mix the flour, baking powder, and salt. Add the sour cream mixture alternately with the flour mixture to the butter mixture, mixing after each addition. Stir in the vanilla.

Turn half the batter into the prepared pan. Spread the pineapple over the batter. Add the remaining batter.

For the topping, combine the granulated sugar, brown sugar, walnuts, cinnamon, and nutmeg.

Sprinkle the topping over the batter and bake for 25 – 30 minutes or until a wooden toothpick inserted in the center comes out clean. Cool on a wire rack.

Cut into squares and serve warm or at room temperature.

***Yield:** 10 – 12 servings*

Hummingbird Cake

3 cups all-purpose flour
2 cups sugar
1 teaspoon baking soda
1 teaspoon ground cinnamon
1 teaspoon salt
1 (8-ounce) can crushed pineapple, undrained
1½ cups vegetable oil
1½ teaspoons vanilla
3 eggs
2 cups diced banana (3 medium)
1 cup chopped pecans

Preheat the oven to 325°F. Grease a 10-inch tube pan.

Combine the flour with the sugar, baking soda, cinnamon, and salt. Add the pineapple, oil, vanilla, eggs, banana, and pecans, mixing by hand until just blended. Turn into the prepared pan.

Bake for 60 minutes or until lightly browned. Cool on a wire rack.

Turn out onto a cake plate and slice. Serve at room temperature.

Yield:* 10 – 12 *servings

Raspberry Breakfast Cake

½ cup softened margarine or butter (¼ pound)
¾ cup sugar
3 eggs
1 small ripe banana, mashed (⅓ cup)
¼ cup milk
¼ cup sour cream
1 teaspoon almond extract
2 cups all-purpose flour
1½ teaspoons baking powder
1½ cups fresh raspberries, or frozen, thawed and drained (¾ pint)

Frosting
1 cup confectioners' sugar
¼ cup softened margarine or butter (⅛ pound)
1 – 2 teaspoons lemon juice

Preheat the oven to 350°F. Grease and flour a 13 x 9 x 2-inch baking pan.

In a large bowl, beat the margarine, sugar, eggs, and banana until light and fluffy. Beat in the milk, sour cream, and almond extract. Stir in the flour and baking powder just until the dry ingredients are moistened.

Turn half the batter into the prepared pan. Sprinkle the raspberries over the batter, then add the remaining batter. Bake for 25 – 30 minutes or until golden brown. Cool on a wire rack while you make the frosting.

Beat the sugar and margarine until well blended. Stir in enough lemon juice for desired spreading consistency. Frost the cake while it is still warm.

Cut into squares and serve warm.

Yield: 10 – 12 servings

Pumpkin Streusel Coffee Cake

Streusel topping
½ cup all-purpose flour
¼ cup brown sugar
1½ teaspoons ground cinnamon
3 tablespoons butter or margarine
½ cup coarsely chopped walnuts

Cake
2 cups all-purpose flour
2 teaspoons baking powder
½ teaspoon baking soda
1½ teaspoons ground cinnamon
¼ teaspoon salt
1 cup softened butter or margarine (½ pound)
1 cup sugar
2 eggs
1 cup solid-packed canned pumpkin
1 teaspoon vanilla

First, make the topping. Combine the flour, brown sugar, and cinnamon in a medium bowl. Cut in the butter with a pastry blender or two knives until the mixture is crumbly. Stir in the walnuts.

Preheat the oven to 350°F. Grease and flour a 13 x 9 x 2-inch baking pan.

To make the cake, combine the flour, baking powder, baking soda, cinnamon, and salt in a small bowl.

Cream the butter and sugar in a large bowl. Add the eggs one at a time, beating well after each addition. Beat in the pumpkin and vanilla. Gradually beat in the flour mixture.

Spoon half the batter into the prepared pan. Sprinkle ¾ cup of the streusel topping over the batter. Spoon the remaining batter evenly over the streusel topping. Sprinkle with the remaining streusel topping.

Bake for 45 – 50 minutes or until a wooden toothpick inserted in the center comes out clean. Cool on a wire rack for 10 minutes, then turn out and cool completely.

Cut into squares and serve at room temperature.

Yield: 10 – 12 servings

Sour Cream-Pecan Coffee Cake

½ cup finely chopped pecans
1½ cups granulated sugar
1½ teaspoons ground cinnamon
¾ cup softened butter, plus 2 tablespoons diced butter or margarine
½ cup brown sugar
3 eggs
2 cups all-purpose flour
1 cup whole wheat flour
1 tablespoon baking powder
¾ teaspoon baking soda
½ teaspoon salt
1½ cups sour cream
1 teaspoon vanilla

Preheat the oven to 350°F. Grease and flour a 10-inch bundt pan.

Combine the pecans, ½ cup of the granulated sugar, and the cinnamon. Spoon 2 tablespoons of this mixture into the prepared pan.

With an electric mixer at medium speed, beat the ¾ cup of softened butter until creamy. Gradually add the remaining cup of granulated sugar and the brown sugar, beating well. Add the eggs one at a time, beating after each addition.

Combine the all-purpose flour, whole wheat flour, baking powder, baking soda, and salt. Add this to the butter mixture alternately with the sour cream, beginning and ending with the flour mixture. Mix after each addition. Stir in the vanilla.

Spoon half the batter into the prepared pan. Sprinkle with half the remaining pecan mixture. Add the remaining batter, spreading evenly, and top with the rest of the pecan mixture. Dot with the 2 tablespoons of diced butter.

Bake for 40 – 45 minutes or until a wooden toothpick inserted in the center comes out clean. Cool on a wire rack for 10 minutes. Turn out onto a cake plate and continue to cool. Cut into slices and serve warm or at room temperature.

Yield: 14 – 16 servings

Poppy Seed Coffee Cake

1 cup buttermilk
6 tablespoons poppy seed
½ teaspoon almond extract
2 cups sugar
1 teaspoon ground cinnamon
1 cup softened butter or margarine (½ pound)
4 eggs, separated
2½ cups all-purpose flour
1 teaspoon baking powder
1 teaspoon baking soda
½ teaspoon salt

Preheat the oven to 350°F. Grease a 10-inch tube pan.

Combine the buttermilk, poppy seed, and almond extract in a small bowl.

Mix ½ cup of the sugar and the cinnamon in a small bowl.

Cream the butter and the remaining 1½ cups of sugar until fluffy. Beat in the egg yolks.

Combine the flour, baking powder, baking soda, and salt. Add to the butter mixture alternately with the buttermilk mixture, beating well after each addition.

Beat the egg whites until soft peaks form. Fold into the batter.

Spoon half the batter into the prepared pan. Sprinkle half the sugar and cinnamon mixture evenly over the batter without letting it touch the sides of the pan. Spoon in the remaining batter and top with the remaining sugar and cinnamon mixture. Bake for 45 minutes or until a wooden toothpick inserted in the center comes out clean. Cool on a wire rack for 5 minutes, then turn out and continue to cool.

Cut into slices and serve warm or at room temperature.

Yield: 10 – 12 servings

Oatmeal Coffee Cake

1 cup quick-cooking rolled oats
½ cup butter (¼ pound)
1¼ cups boiling water
2 eggs, beaten
1⅓ cups all-purpose flour
1 teaspoon baking soda
1 cup brown sugar
1 cup granulated sugar
1 teaspoon ground cinnamon
1 teaspoon ground nutmeg
Dash of salt

Topping
1 cup brown sugar
½ cup butter, melted (¼ pound)
¼ cup milk
1 cup sweetened flaked coconut
1 cup chopped pecans
1 teaspoon vanilla

Preheat the oven to 350°F. Grease and flour a 13 x 9 x 2-inch baking pan.

First make the cake. Put the rolled oats in a large bowl and place the butter on top. Cover with the boiling water and let stand for 20 minutes.

Mix the beaten eggs, flour, baking soda, brown sugar, granulated sugar, cinnamon, nutmeg, and salt. Stir into the oatmeal mixture. Turn into the prepared pan and bake for 35 minutes or until a wooden toothpick inserted in the center comes out clean. Cool on a wire rack.

To make the topping, mix the sugar, butter, and milk. Stir in the coconut, pecans, and vanilla. Spread over the cake and broil for 2 – 3 minutes or until the topping begins to brown.

Cut into squares and serve warm or at room temperature.

***Yield:** 10 – 12 servings*

Sandwiches, Savories, & Spreads

Creamy Lemon-Pecan Sandwiches

3 egg yolks
½ cup sugar
Juice of 3 lemons
Zest of 3 lemons, grated
8 ounces softened cream cheese
1 cup chopped pecans
12 slices date-nut or whole wheat bread

Cook the egg yolks, sugar, and lemon juice over medium heat, stirring constantly, until thickened. Stir in the grated zest. Cool. Mix in the cream cheese and pecans.

Spread half the bread slices with this mixture. Cover with the remaining slices.

Trim the crusts. Cut each sandwich diagonally to make 4 triangular tea sandwiches.

Yield: 24 sandwiches

Cheese and Walnut Sandwiches

½ cup butter (¼ pound)
1 cup grated sharp Cheddar cheese (4 ounces)
½ teaspoon Dijon mustard
Dash of cayenne
Dash of Worcestershire sauce
¾ cup – 1 cup chopped walnuts, toasted
12 thin slices firm white bread

With a heavy-duty electric mixer or in a food processor, cream the butter, cheese, mustard, cayenne, and Worcestershire sauce until smooth. Stir in the walnuts by hand.

Spread half the bread slices thinly with the mixture. Cover with the remaining slices.

Trim the crusts. Cut each sandwich diagonally to make 4 triangular tea sandwiches.

Yield: 24 sandwiches

Chutney and Cheese Sandwiches

This cheese mixture can also be served as a spread for crackers.

8 ounces softened cream cheese
2 cups grated sharp Cheddar cheese (8 ounces)
½ cup Major Grey chutney (see note)
2 teaspoons prepared mustard
2 tablespoons snipped fresh chives, or 2 teaspoons dried
1 loaf dense multigrain bread, thinly sliced (26 – 28 slices)
Softened butter
½ cup finely chopped walnuts

In a food processor, blend the cream cheese, Cheddar cheese, chutney, mustard, and chives until smooth.

Spread half the bread slices evenly with the cheese mixture. Cover with the remaining slices.

Trim the crusts. Cut each sandwich diagonally to make 4 triangular tea sandwiches.

Spread a little butter over two cut edges of each sandwich and dip into the chopped walnuts.

Cover with a damp tea towel until ready to serve.

Note: Major Grey is a type of chutney made with mangos. There are many different brands of Major Grey chutney.

Yield: 52 – 56 sandwiches (or 2 cups of spread)

Watercress Sandwiches

½ cup chopped watercress
6 tablespoons softened butter
8 slices firm white bread

Combine the watercress and butter and spread half the bread slices evenly with this mixture. Cover with the remaining slices.

Trim the crusts. Cut each sandwich diagonally to make 4 triangular tea sandwiches.

Yield: 16 sandwiches

Cucumber Sandwiches

4 ounces commercial cream cheese with chives
12 slices firm white bread
2 cucumbers, peeled and thinly sliced

Spread half the bread slices evenly with the cream cheese. Top with the sliced cucumber. Cover with the remaining slices.

Trim the crusts. Cut each sandwich diagonally to make 4 triangular tea sandwiches.

Yield: 24 sandwiches

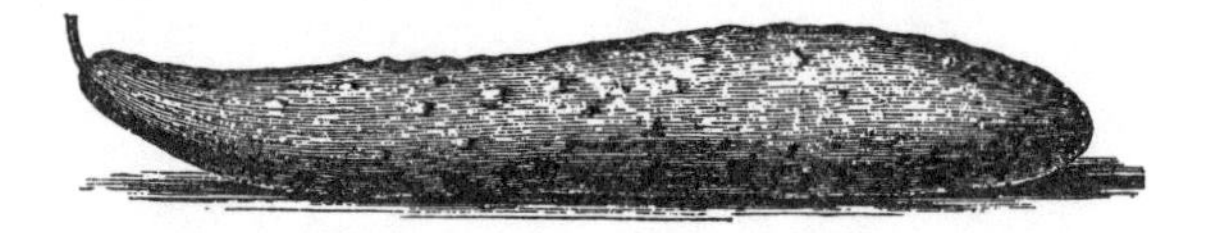

Shrimp-Cucumber Rounds

8 slices whole wheat bread
1 (4-ounce) package commercial garlic-and-herb cheese spread
1 cucumber, scored with a fork and sliced
1 (4½-ounce) can small shrimp, drained and rinsed

Using a 2-inch cookie cutter, cut the bread into 24 rounds.

Spread each with 1 teaspoon of the cheese spread. Top with 1 slice of cucumber and 1 small shrimp. If necessary, add a bit of cheese spread to the top of each cucumber slice to secure the shrimp.

Yield: 24 open-faced sandwiches

Miniature BLT Sandwiches

8 slices firm white bread
6 strips bacon, cooked and crumbled
⅓ cup mayonnaise
Green leaf lettuce
4 plum tomatoes, thinly sliced

Using a 2-inch cookie cutter, cut the bread into 24 rounds.

Blend the bacon with the mayonnaise and spread the mixture over the bread rounds. Place a piece of lettuce on each and top with a slice of tomato.

Yield: 24 open-faced sandwiches

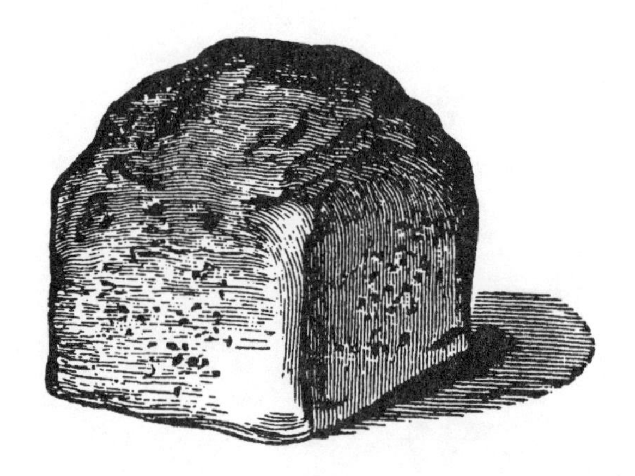

Seasoned Crackers

The Carroll family has been enjoying these tasty low-fat snacks for many years.

¾ cup vegetable oil
½ teaspoon lemon pepper
½ teaspoon garlic powder
¼ teaspoon dried dill weed
1 small package powdered ranch-style salad dressing mix
1 (11-ounce) package oyster crackers

Mix all the ingredients except the crackers. Place the crackers in a bowl and drizzle the mixture over them. Blend well. Dry on paper towels.

Note: Store at room temperature in a plastic container or glass jar.

Yield: 20 servings

Cheese-Straw Daisy Crackers

2 cups grated sharp Cheddar cheese, at room temperature (8 ounces)
½ cup butter (¼ pound)
½ cup vegetable shortening
⅓ cup grated Romano cheese (1½ ounces)
1 tablespoon water
2 teaspoons salt
¼ teaspoon cayenne
2 (rounded) cups all-purpose flour
1 teaspoon baking powder

Preheat the oven to 375°F.

In a food processor, cream the Cheddar cheese, butter, shortening, Romano cheese, water, salt, and cayenne.

Combine the flour and baking powder and slowly mix this into the cheese mixture.

Place in a pastry bag with a large star tip and squeeze onto an ungreased baking sheet.

Bake for 15 minutes or until crisp.

Yield: 70 – 80 daisy crackers

Feta Cheese Cups

This recipe was given to me by my aunt, Betty Carter, a fabulous cook.

8 slices firm white bread
¼ cup butter, melted (⅛ pound)
1 large egg, beaten
3 ounces softened cream cheese
¾ cup crumbled feta cheese (3 ounces)

Preheat the oven to 350°F. Grease 24 miniature muffin cups.

Using a 2-inch cookie cutter, cut the bread into rounds to fit the muffin cups. Brush one side of the bread with the melted butter and fit it into the muffin cup buttered side down.

Combine the egg, cream cheese, and feta cheese. Drop 1 teaspoon of the cheese mixture into each muffin cup.

Bake for 20 minutes or until puffy and lightly browned.

Yield: 24 cheese cups

Savory Stuffed Celery

8 ounces cream cheese
¼ cup Major Grey chutney (see note)
¼ teaspoon powdered mustard
1 teaspoon curry powder
½ cup chopped pecans
10 – 12 stalks celery, cut into 1½-inch lengths

In a food processor, blend the cream cheese, chutney, mustard, and curry powder. Scrape the mixture into a medium bowl and fold in the pecans.

Stuff each piece of celery with 2 teaspoonfuls of the cheese spread.

Refrigerate for 60 minutes before serving.

(Before stuffing the celery, you can refrigerate the cheese spread, covered in plastic wrap, for up to a week.)

Note: Major Grey is a type of chutney made with mangos. There are many different brands of Major Grey chutney.

Yield: 60 bite-sized pieces

Miniature Quiches

Pastry
1 cup softened butter (½ pound)
8 ounces softened cream cheese
2 cups all-purpose flour
½ teaspoon salt

Filling
1 medium onion, chopped (⅔ cup)
2 tablespoons butter
2½ cups finely grated Swiss cheese (10 ounces)
3 eggs
1½ cups half-and-half
½ teaspoon salt
Dash of pepper
Dash of ground nutmeg

First, make the pastry. Preheat the oven to 350°F. Grease 60 miniature muffin cups.

Combine the butter, cream cheese, flour, and salt until well blended. Roll into balls and press into the prepared miniature muffin cups. Bake for 3 – 5 minutes.

Next, make the filling. Sauté the onion in the butter until transparent.

Place a teaspoon of the Swiss cheese in each pastry shell.

Blend the eggs, cream, salt, pepper, and nutmeg. Mix in the onion. Place 1 teaspoon of the egg mixture over the cheese in each pastry shell, filling two thirds full.

Bake in a 350°F oven for 20 minutes or until set and lightly browned.

Yield: 60 miniature quiches

Blue Cheese-Pecan Grapes

1 cup crumbled blue cheese (4 ounces)
3 ounces softened cream cheese
¼ pound seedless green grapes (about 24 grapes)
1 cup finely chopped pecans

Using an electric mixer at medium speed, beat the blue cheese and cream cheese until smooth. Refrigerate for at least 60 minutes.

Encase each grape in the cheese mixture. Roll each grape in the pecans.

Refrigerate again for at least 60 minutes.

Yield: 8 servings

Islander Cheese Ball

1 pound softened cream cheese
1 (8-ounce) can crushed pineapple, drained
¼ – ½ cup chopped green pepper (¼ – ½ small)
2 tablespoons chopped scallions (including green tops)
2 teaspoons seasoned salt
2 cups chopped pecans

Mix the cream cheese and pineapple using an electric mixer. Stir in the green pepper, scallions, salt, and ½ cup of the pecans.

Roll into a large ball or two logs — or, alternatively, fill a scooped-out pineapple half.

Top with the remaining 1½ cups of pecans. Chill.

Note: This can be refrigerated, covered with plastic wrap, for up to a week.

Yield: 2 cups

Walnut-Date Cheese Ball

⅔ cup chopped dates
8 ounces sharp Cheddar cheese, cut into 1-inch pieces
8 ounces softened cream cheese, cut into 1-inch pieces
2 tablespoons rum
⅔ cup coarsely chopped walnuts

In a food processor, combine the dates, Cheddar cheese, cream cheese, and rum and process for 1 minute.

Form into a ball and refrigerate for several hours.

Press the walnuts onto the top and sides of the cheese ball. Serve with crackers and apple and pear slices.

Note: This can be refrigerated, in a tightly sealed container, for up to 2 weeks.

Yield: 2 cups

Shrimp Butter

8 ounces cream cheese
½ cup butter (¼ pound)
¼ cup mayonnaise
Juice of 1 lemon
1 tablespoon minced onion
Salt to taste
2 (5-ounce) cans shrimp, coarsely chopped

In a food processor, combine the cream cheese, butter, mayonnaise, lemon juice, onion, and salt. Add the shrimp and process briefly.

Rinse a mold or bowl in cold water. Grease the mold, then turn the shrimp butter into it. Chill.

Unmold and serve with crackers.

Note: This can be refrigerated, in a tightly sealed container, for up to 3 days.

Yield: 2 cups

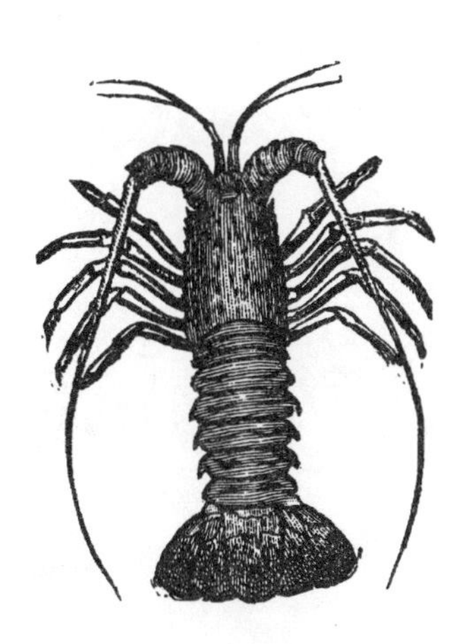

Apple and Cheese Spread

8 ounces cream cheese
1 cup grated sharp Cheddar cheese (4 ounces)
½ cup mayonnaise
¼ cup sugar
1 medium red apple, cored and finely chopped but not peeled (1 cup)
½ cup finely chopped celery
Chopped walnuts

Mix all the ingredients except the walnuts. Form into a mound on a plate and top with the walnuts. Chill.

Serve with crackers or as a sandwich spread.

Note: This can be refrigerated, covered with plastic wrap, for up to a week.

Yield: 2 cups

Tangy Orange-Cheese Spread

8 ounces softened cream cheese
¼ cup confectioners' sugar
1 tablespoon grated orange zest
1 tablespoon orange-flavored liqueur
1 tablespoon frozen orange juice concentrate, thawed

Blend all the ingredients in a food processor.

Serve with crackers or as a sandwich spread.

Note: This can be refrigerated, in a tightly sealed container, for up to 2 weeks.

Yield: 1 cup

Cheddar Cheese and Nut Spread

3 cups grated sharp Cheddar cheese (12 ounces)
8 ounces softened cream cheese, cut crosswise into 4 even chunks
2 tablespoons milk
½ cup crumbled blue cheese (2 ounces)
¼ cup chopped walnuts
Chopped parsley

Using plastic wrap, line four (6-ounce) custard cups or crocks, letting the wrap hang over the sides.

Process half the Cheddar cheese, 1 chunk of the cream cheese, and 1 tablespoon of the milk in a food processor until smooth. Scrape the mixture into a medium bowl. Repeat with the remaining Cheddar cheese, another chunk of the cream cheese, and the remaining milk.

In a small bowl, blend the remaining 2 chunks of cream cheese, the blue cheese, and the walnuts.

Distribute half the Cheddar cheese mixture into the prepared custard cups. Top with the blue cheese mixture, then the remaining Cheddar cheese mixture. Cover with the overhanging wrap.

Refrigerate for at least 4 hours, or until firm.

Unwrap and unmold onto a serving plate. Serve garnished with the parsley.

Note: This can be refrigerated, covered with plastic wrap, for up to 2 weeks.

Yield: 4 cups

Cheese and Olive Spread

8 ounces cream cheese, at room temperature
1½ cups crumbled blue cheese, at room temperature (6 ounces)
½ cup butter, at room temperature (¼ pound), plus extra for frying
1 cup coarsely chopped ripe olives
3 tablespoons snipped fresh chives
2 tablespoons brandy
⅓ cup slivered almonds

In a food processor, thoroughly mix the cream cheese, blue cheese, butter, olives, chives, and brandy. Shape into a mound on a serving plate and chill.

In a frying pan over medium heat, toast the almonds in a small amount of butter until golden, stirring often. Arrange the almonds over the chilled cheese mound.

Serve with crackers or melba toast.

Note: This can be refrigerated, in a tightly sealed container, for up to 2 weeks.

Yield: 2 cups

Savory Cheese Spread

1 pound softened cream cheese
1½ cups crumbled feta cheese (6 ounces)
¼ cup fresh parsley
1 tablespoon snipped fresh chives, or 2 teaspoons dried
2 teaspoons chopped fresh thyme, or 1 teaspoon dried
⅛ teaspoon coarsely ground black pepper
1 clove garlic
½ cup finely chopped ripe olives

In a food processor, blend all the ingredients except the olives. Stir in the olives and spoon into a serving bowl.

Serve with assorted crackers.

Note: This can be refrigerated, in a tightly sealed container, for up to a week.

Yield: 2¾ cups

Christmas Cheese Spread

½ cup stuffed green olives, chopped
1 small green pepper, chopped (1 cup)
1 small red pepper, chopped (1 cup)
¼ cup chopped fresh parsley
1½ cups crumbled blue cheese (6 ounces)
1 cup butter (½ pound)
8 ounces cream cheese
1 teaspoon paprika
2 drops Tabasco sauce
1 teaspoon Worcestershire sauce

Mix the olives and green and red peppers with the parsley.

In a food processor, combine the blue cheese, butter, and cream cheese. Add the paprika, Tabasco sauce, and Worcestershire sauce and process briefly. Stir in the olive mixture. Form into a loaf and chill.

Serve with crackers.

Note: This can be refrigerated, in a tightly sealed container, for up to a week.

Yield:* *2 cups

Layered Pesto Spread

1 cup whole fresh basil leaves, plus extra for garnish
⅓ cup grated Parmesan cheese (1⅓ ounces)
2 tablespoons olive oil
½ cup pine nuts
1 (8-ounce) container whipped cream cheese

Line a small bowl with plastic wrap.

Chop the 1 cup of basil in a food processor. Blend in the Parmesan cheese and olive oil. Stir in the pine nuts by hand.

Layer the whipped cream cheese and the basil pesto alternately in the lined bowl, beginning and ending with the cream cheese. Refrigerate for 60 minutes.

Invert onto a serving plate and remove the plastic wrap.

Garnish with the extra basil leaves and serve with crackers.

Note: This can be refrigerated, in a tightly sealed container, for up to 2 weeks.

Yield: 1½ cups

Drop Cookies & Bar Cookies

Chocolate Chip Meringues

2 egg whites
1 teaspoon vanilla
¼ teaspoon cream of tartar
¼ teaspoon salt
¾ cup sugar
1 cup semisweet chocolate chips (6 ounces)

Preheat the oven to 300°F. Line a baking sheet with parchment paper.

Beat the egg whites, vanilla, cream of tartar, and salt until soft peaks form. Gradually beat in the sugar until the mixture is very stiff and glossy. Fold in the chocolate chips.

Drop the dough by the teaspoonful onto the prepared baking sheet and bake for 15 – 25 minutes or until the cookies are set and lightly browned. Cool on wire racks.

Yield: 24 meringues

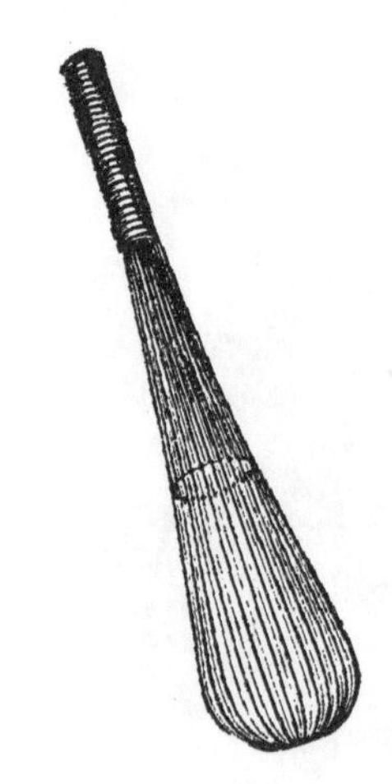

Brown Sugar Meringues

4 egg whites
1 tablespoon cornstarch
1 teaspoon vanilla
¼ teaspoon almond extract
2 cups brown sugar
1 cup chopped pecans

Preheat the oven to 300°F. Line two or three baking sheets with parchment paper.

Beat the egg whites, cornstarch, vanilla, and almond extract until frothy. Gradually add the sugar, beating until stiff peaks form. Fold in the pecans.

Drop by the heaping teaspoonful onto the prepared baking sheets and bake for 25 minutes or until firm to the touch. Cool on wire racks.

Yield: 36 meringues

Ambrosia Cookies

This recipe calls for the dough to be refrigerated for 2 hours before baking.

½ cup butter (¼ pound)
½ cup vegetable shortening
1 cup brown sugar
1 cup granulated sugar
2 eggs
1 tablespoon grated orange zest
2 cups all-purpose flour
1 teaspoon baking powder
½ teaspoon baking soda
½ teaspoon salt
3 tablespoons orange juice
1½ cups large-flake rolled oats
3 cups sweetened flaked coconut

Preheat the oven to 375°F.

Cream the butter and shortening. Gradually add the brown sugar and granulated sugar, beating until light. Add the eggs and the orange zest and beat well.

Combine the flour, baking powder, baking soda, and salt. Add this to the creamed mixture alternately with the orange juice, mixing after each addition. Stir in the rolled oats and coconut.

Refrigerate the dough for 2 hours. Drop by the teaspoonful onto four ungreased baking sheets and bake for 12 minutes or until lightly browned. Cool on wire racks.

Yield: 8 dozen cookies

Easiest Sugar Cookies

⅓ cup softened margarine or butter (⅙ pound)
¾ cup sugar, plus 2 tablespoons white or colored sugar
⅓ cup vegetable oil
1 tablespoon milk
1 – 2 teaspoons almond extract
1 egg
1½ cups all-purpose flour
1½ teaspoons baking powder
¼ teaspoon salt

Preheat the oven to 375°F.

In a large bowl, beat the margarine, ¾ cup sugar, oil, milk, almond extract, and egg until light and fluffy.

Stir the flour, baking powder, and salt into the margarine mixture and blend well.

Spread evenly in an ungreased 15 x 10 x 1-inch jelly roll pan. Sprinkle with the 2 tablespoons of sugar and bake for 10 – 12 minutes or until golden.

Cool on a wire rack for 5 minutes and then cut into rectangular cookies.

Yield: 48 cookies

Ginger Cookies

This recipe calls for the dough to be refrigerated for 90 minutes before baking.

1 cup brown sugar
¾ cup vegetable shortening
1 egg, beaten
¼ cup molasses
2¼ cups all-purpose flour
1½ teaspoons baking soda
½ teaspoon salt
1 teaspoon ground ginger
1 teaspoon ground cinnamon
½ teaspoon ground cloves
Granulated sugar

Preheat the oven to 350°F. Grease three baking sheets.

Slowly cream the brown sugar with the shortening. Blend in the egg and molasses.

Combine the flour, baking soda, salt, ginger, cinnamon, and cloves. Add this to the brown sugar mixture, stirring until just blended. Refrigerate the dough for 90 minutes.

Mold the dough into 1-inch balls. Dip the bottom of a drinking glass into the granulated sugar and use it to flatten the balls onto the prepared baking sheets.

Bake for 7 – 10 minutes or until crisp. Cool on wire racks.

Yield: 6 dozen cookies

Stained-Glass Heart Cookies

For this recipe, you will need one large and one small heart-shaped cookie cutter. Note that the dough must be chilled before baking.

½ cup butter (¼ pound)
1 cup sugar
1 egg
2 cups all-purpose flour
2 teaspoons baking powder
½ teaspoon salt
½ teaspoon vanilla
1 cup red hard candy, crushed

Cream the butter and sugar. Blend in the egg.

Combine the flour, baking powder, and salt and add to the butter mixture, stirring just until combined. Blend in the vanilla. Chill the dough thoroughly.

Preheat the oven to 400°F. Line three baking sheets with foil.

Roll out the dough to a thickness of an eighth of an inch. Using a large heart-shaped cookie cutter, cut out the cookies and place them on the prepared baking sheets. Using a small heart-shaped cookie cutter, cut out and remove the centers of the large hearts (these can be baked and decorated separately). Fill the centers with the crushed candy.

Bake for 8 minutes or until the cookies are lightly browned and the candy is melted. Cool on wire racks. Carefully loosen the cookies from the foil when cool.

Yield: 36 cookies

Christmas Wreath Cookies

2 cups butter, at room temperature (1 pound)
2 cups sugar
1 egg
1 teaspoon vanilla
3½ cups all-purpose flour
½ cup cornstarch
Green food coloring
Red candy bits or baking decorations

Preheat the oven to 350°F.

Using an electric mixer, cream the butter and sugar until light and fluffy. Mix in the egg and vanilla. Add the flour and cornstarch and mix until just blended. Stir in the food coloring.

Transfer the dough to a cookie press with a star tip. To make uniform wreaths, press the dough out in long strips. Using a knife, cut the dough into 2½-inch lengths. Form each length into a ring. Overlap the ends slightly and press gently.

Place the wreaths on three ungreased baking sheets. Decorate them with red candy bits or baking decorations so that they resemble wreaths of holly.

Bake for 10 minutes or until firm to the touch. Do not allow the cookies to brown. Cool on wire racks.

Yield: 6 dozen wreaths

Orange Shortbread

1 cup softened butter (½ pound)
¾ cup confectioners' sugar
1 teaspoon grated orange zest
2 teaspoons frozen orange juice concentrate, thawed
1¾ cups all-purpose flour
Sliced almonds

Preheat the oven to 300°F. Lightly grease a 15 x 10 x 1-inch jelly roll pan.

Beat the butter with an electric mixer set at medium speed. Add the sugar gradually, beating well. Beat in the orange zest and orange juice concentrate. Stir in the flour.

Press the dough into the prepared pan and prick all over with a fork. Cut into 1½-inch diamonds and place an almond slice in the center of each.

Bake for 30 minutes or until lightly browned.

Recut the diamonds while warm. Cool in the pan on a wire rack.

Yield: 48 cookies

Spiced Shortbread

1 cup softened butter (½ pound)
½ cup sugar
½ teaspoon almond extract
½ teaspoon ground nutmeg
2 cups all-purpose flour

Preheat the oven to 350°F. Grease a 13 x 9 x 2-inch baking pan.

Using an electric mixer or a food processor, beat the butter and sugar until light and fluffy. Add the almond extract and nutmeg and mix briefly. Gradually add the flour, a half cup at a time, mixing thoroughly after each addition.

Press the dough into the prepared pan and bake for 20 minutes or until lightly browned.

Cut into square cookies while hot. Cool on a wire rack.

Yield: 36 cookies

Raisin-Walnut Shortbread Bars

1¼ cups all-purpose flour
½ cup granulated sugar
½ cup butter or margarine (¼ pound)
2 eggs
½ cup brown sugar
1 teaspoon vanilla
⅛ teaspoon baking soda
1 cup chopped walnuts
1 cup raisins
½ cup sweetened flaked coconut (optional)

Preheat the oven to 350°F. Lightly grease an 8-inch-square baking pan.

Combine the flour and granulated sugar. Using a pastry blender or two knives, cut in the butter until the mixture resembles fine meal. Press into the prepared pan and bake for 20 minutes or until the edges are golden.

Meanwhile, combine the eggs, brown sugar, and vanilla. Beat well. Stir in the baking soda, walnuts, raisins, and coconut. Spread evenly over the hot crust.

Return to the oven and bake for an additional 20 – 25 minutes or until the top is set.

Cool on a wire rack and cut into bars.

Yield: 16 bars

Granola Bars

½ cup butter (¼ pound)
1 cup graham cracker crumbs
1 cup plain granola
1 (14-ounce) can sweetened condensed milk
1 cup butterscotch bits (6 ounces)
1 cup chopped nuts

Preheat the oven to 350°F.

Melt the butter in a 13 x 9 x 2-inch baking pan. Sprinkle with the graham cracker crumbs, then the granola. Drizzle the milk on top. Scatter the butterscotch bits and the nuts over the top.

Bake for 30 minutes or until slightly browned. Cool on a wire rack and cut into bars.

Yield: 36 bars

Apricot Oatmeal Bars

1½ cups all-purpose flour
1 teaspoon baking powder
½ teaspoon salt
1½ cups large-flake rolled oats
1 cup light brown sugar
¾ cup chilled butter, cut into bits
1 (10-ounce) jar apricot preserves

Preheat the oven to 350°F. Grease well a 13 x 9 x 2-inch baking pan.

Combine the flour, baking powder, and salt in a large bowl. Add the rolled oats, sugar, and butter. Blend until the mixture resembles meal.

Press half the mixture into the prepared pan. Spread the preserves over all. Sprinkle the remaining mixture over the preserves.

Bake for 30 minutes or until lightly browned. Cool on a wire rack and cut into bars.

Yield: 36 bars

Chocolate Oatmeal Bars

FILLING
2 tablespoons butter
1 cup chocolate chips (6 ounces)
1 (5⅓-ounce) can evaporated milk
¼ cup sugar
½ cup chopped walnuts

BASE
½ cup butter (¼ pound)
1 cup brown sugar
1 egg
1 teaspoon vanilla
1¼ cups all-purpose flour
½ teaspoon baking soda
2 cups quick-cooking rolled oats

Preheat the oven to 350°F. Grease a 9-inch-square baking pan.

First, make the filling. In a heavy saucepan, combine the butter, chocolate chips, milk, and sugar. Bring to a boil, stirring constantly. Remove from heat and stir in the walnuts. Cool.

To prepare the base, cream the butter and sugar. Add the egg and vanilla, beating until light and fluffy. Stir in the flour, baking soda, and 1¾ cups of the rolled oats until well blended. Press two thirds of this base mixture into the bottom of the prepared pan. Spread with the cooled filling. Mix the remaining ¼ cup of rolled oats with the remaining base mixture and crumble over the filling.

Bake for 25 minutes or until a wooden toothpick inserted in the center comes out clean. Cool on a wire rack and cut into bars.

Yield: 24 bars

Chocolate Streusel Bars

1¾ cups all-purpose flour
1½ cups confectioners' sugar
½ cups unsweetened cocoa powder
1 cup chilled butter (½ pound)
8 ounces softened cream cheese
1 (14-ounce) can sweetened condensed milk
1 egg
2 teaspoons vanilla
½ cup chopped walnuts

Preheat the oven to 350°F. Grease a 13 x 9 x 2-inch baking pan.

In a large bowl, combine the flour, sugar, and cocoa. With a pastry blender or two knives, cut in the butter until crumbly (the mixture will be dry).

Reserve 2 cups of the mixture and press the remainder onto the bottom of the prepared baking pan. Bake for 15 minutes.

In a large bowl, beat the cream cheese until fluffy. Add the milk gradually, beating until smooth. Add the egg and vanilla and mix well. Turn into the baked crust.

Stir the walnuts into the reserved crumb mixture and sprinkle evenly over the batter.

Bake for 20 minutes or until bubbly and lightly browned. Cool on a wire rack and cut into bars.

Note: Store covered in the refrigerator.

Yield: 36 bars

Fruity Chocolate Dream Bars

1¼ cups all-purpose flour
½ cup sugar
½ cup softened butter (¼ pound)
½ cup seedless raspberry jam (or jam or jelly of choice)
1½ cups semisweet chocolate chips (9 ounces)

TOPPING
⅔ cup all-purpose flour
6 tablespoons softened butter
6 tablespoons sugar
½ cup chopped pecans
½ teaspoon vanilla

Preheat the oven to 350°F. Grease a 13 x 9 x 2-inch baking pan.

Combine the flour and the sugar. With a pastry blender or two knives, cut in the butter until the mixture resembles fine crumbs. Press into the prepared pan and bake for 20 – 25 minutes.

Carefully spread the jam over the baked crust. Top with the chocolate chips.

To make the topping, mix the flour, butter, sugar, pecans, and vanilla with a fork until the mixture resembles coarse crumbs. Sprinkle over the chocolate chips and bake for 15 – 20 minutes or until lightly browned.

Cool on a wire rack and cut into bars.

Yield: 36 bars

Pumpkin Spice Bars

4 eggs
2 cups sugar
1 cup vegetable oil
1 (16-ounce) can solid-packed pumpkin
2 cups all-purpose flour
2 teaspoons baking powder
1 teaspoon baking soda
¾ teaspoon salt
2 teaspoons ground cinnamon
½ teaspoon ground ginger
¼ teaspoon ground cloves
½ cup raisins

FROSTING
3 ounces softened cream cheese
6 tablespoons softened margarine or butter
1 teaspoon vanilla
2 cups confectioners' sugar

Preheat the oven to 350°F. Grease a 15 x 10 x 1-inch jelly roll pan.

Beat the eggs, sugar, oil, and pumpkin. Stir in the flour, baking powder, baking soda, salt, cinnamon, ginger, cloves, and raisins.

Turn into the prepared pan and bake for 25 – 30 minutes or until the top springs back when pressed with a finger. Cool on a wire rack.

To make the frosting, mix the cream cheese, margarine, and vanilla. Gradually beat in the sugar until smooth and of spreading consistency. Spread over the cooled base, then cut into bars.

Yield: 48 bars

Strawberry Bars

¾ cup softened butter or margarine
1 cup sugar
2 egg yolks
1 teaspoon vanilla
2 cups all-purpose flour
2 teaspoons baking powder
½ teaspoon salt
1 cup chopped pecans
½ cup strawberry jam

Preheat the oven to 325°F. Grease a 9-inch-square baking pan.

Cream the butter. Add the sugar gradually, beating until light and fluffy. Add the egg yolks and the vanilla, beating well. Gradually stir in the flour, baking powder, salt, and pecans.

Pat half the dough into the prepared pan. Spread the strawberry jam evenly over the dough. Drop the remaining dough by the tablespoonful over the jam; spread evenly.

Bake for 45 minutes or until lightly browned. Cool on a wire rack and cut into bars.

Yield: 24 bars

Linzer Bars

3¼ cups all-purpose flour
1½ cups sugar
1 cup butter (½ pound)
1 teaspoon baking powder
½ teaspoon salt
¾ cup chopped slivered almonds
1 teaspoon grated lemon zest
2 eggs, beaten
1 (12-ounce) jar seedless raspberry jam

Preheat the oven to 375°F. Grease a 15 x 10 x 1-inch jelly roll pan.

Place 3 cups of the flour, the sugar, butter, baking powder, salt, and almonds in a large bowl. Using an electric mixer set at low speed, beat until crumbly. Add the lemon zest and eggs and stir with a fork until the mixture is evenly moistened.

Reserve 1 cup of the dough and pat the remainder into the prepared pan. Spread the jam over the dough.

Combine the remaining ¼ cup of flour with the reserved 1 cup of dough. Sprinkle this mixture evenly over the layer of jam.

Bake for 25 minutes or until lightly browned. Cool on a wire rack and cut into bars.

Yield: 48 bars

California Blondies

These bars must be made at least 8 hours before the glaze is applied.

1¼ cups all-purpose flour
1¼ teaspoons baking powder
½ teaspoon salt
⅔ cup softened butter (⅓ pound)
½ cup granulated sugar
⅔ cup light brown sugar
1 teaspoon vanilla
2 teaspoons grated orange zest
1 teaspoon grated lemon zest
2 eggs
2 teaspoons milk
1 cup slivered, blanched almonds

Glaze

2 tablespoons softened butter
½ cup confectioners' sugar
2 teaspoons frozen orange juice concentrate, thawed
1 tablespoon milk or half-and-half

Preheat the oven to 350°F. Grease a 9-inch-square baking pan.

Combine the flour, baking powder, and salt in a small bowl. Stir to mix well.

Beat the butter and granulated sugar until light and fluffy. Beat in the brown sugar until well blended. Add the vanilla, orange zest, and lemon zest. Mix well. Add the eggs one at a time, beating well after each addition. Blend in the milk. Fold in the flour mixture and the almonds.

Spread evenly in the prepared pan and bake for 30 – 35 minutes or until a wooden toothpick inserted in the center comes out barely moist.

Cool completely in the pan on a wire rack. Cover with aluminum foil and let stand at room temperature for at least 8 hours, or overnight.

To make the glaze, beat the butter, sugar, orange juice concentrate, and milk until the mixture is smooth and creamy and of spreading consistency.

Cut the bars and garnish each with a dab of glaze.

Yield: 24 bars

Cranberry-Orange Bars

1 (10-ounce) jar commercial cranberry-orange relish
1 tablespoon cornstarch
1 teaspoon ground ginger
½ cup chopped walnuts
1½ cups confectioners' sugar
1 cup softened margarine or butter (½ pound)
1 egg
1 teaspoon vanilla
½ teaspoon almond extract
2½ cups all-purpose flour

GLAZE
1 cup confectioners' sugar
½ teaspoon vanilla
2 tablespoons milk

In a small saucepan, bring the relish, cornstarch, and ginger to a boil over medium heat, stirring constantly. Boil, stirring, for 1 minute. Remove from heat and stir in the walnuts. Cool.

Preheat the oven to 350°F. Grease a 13 x 9 x 2-inch baking pan.

Mix the sugar, margarine, egg, vanilla, and almond extract. Stir in the flour. Reserve 1 cup of the dough and press the remainder into the prepared baking pan. Spread the relish mixture over the dough. Drop the reserved dough by the scant teaspoonful onto the relish mixture.

Bake for 35 minutes or until a wooden toothpick inserted in the center comes out clean. Cool on a wire rack.

Meanwhile, make the glaze. Mix the sugar and vanilla. Stir in the milk, 1 teaspoonful at a time, until the glaze is smooth and of spreading consistency. Drizzle the glaze onto the cooled base, then cut into bars.

Yield: 36 bars

Lemon-Frosted Pecan Bars

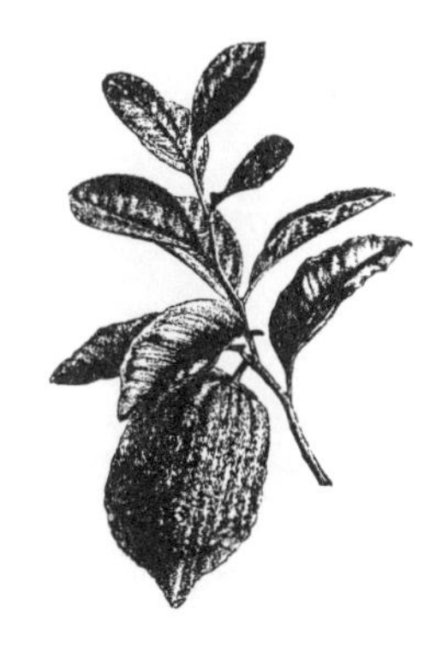

1¾ cups all-purpose flour
⅓ cup confectioners' sugar
¾ cup butter
2 cups brown sugar
4 eggs, beaten
1 cup chopped pecans
½ teaspoon baking powder

FROSTING
¾ cup softened butter
3 cups confectioners' sugar
1½ teaspoons grated lemon zest
2 tablespoons fresh lemon juice

Preheat the oven to 350°F. Grease a 13 x 9 x 2-inch baking pan.

Combine 1½ cups of the flour with the confectioners' sugar. Cut in the butter with a pastry blender or two knives until the mixture is crumbly. Press onto the bottom of the prepared pan and bake for 15 minutes.

Meanwhile, in a large bowl combine the brown sugar, the remaining ¼ cup of flour, the eggs, pecans, and baking powder. Mix well. Spread evenly over the baked crust and bake for 20 – 25 minutes or until lightly browned. Cool.

Next, prepare the frosting. Using an electric mixer, beat the butter, sugar, lemon zest, and lemon juice until well blended and of spreading consistency.

Spread the frosting over the cooled base, then cut into bars.

Yield: 36 bars

Easy Lemon Bars

1 (14-ounce) can sweetened condensed milk
2 tablespoons grated lemon zest
¼ cup lemon juice
2 cups all-purpose flour
1 cup sugar
¾ cup softened butter
¼ teaspoon salt
½ cup sweetened flaked coconut

Preheat the oven to 375°F. Grease a 13 x 9 x 2-inch baking pan.

Mix the milk, lemon zest, and lemon juice until thick.

Mix the flour, sugar, butter, and salt until the mixture is crumbly. Reserve 1½ cups and press the remainder firmly into the prepared pan. Spoon the milk mixture over the top and spread carefully to cover.

Mix the coconut into the reserved flour mixture. Sprinkle this evenly over the batter and press lightly. Bake for 25 – 30 minutes or until golden brown.

Cool on a wire rack and cut into bars.

Yield: 36 bars

Confection Date Bars

½ cup butter (¼ pound)
¾ cup granulated sugar
1 egg
1⅓ cups buttermilk baking mix (see note)
½ cup chopped walnuts
1 cup chopped dates
Confectioners' sugar

Preheat the oven to 350°F. Grease an 8-inch-square baking pan.

Cream the butter, granulated sugar, and egg. Stir in the buttermilk baking mix, walnuts, and dates. Turn into the prepared pan and bake for 25 minutes.

Cool on a wire rack and cut into bars. Dust with the confectioners' sugar.

Note: I use Bisquick brand in this recipe, with good results.

Yield:* *16 bars

Time assassinating,
To verandas drawn,
Lounging in pavilion,
Smoking on the lawn;
Gossip, cobblers, romance,
Flirting and croquet,
Till darkness drops its mantle
O'er nature at Cape May.

Squares & Cupcakes

Sinful Brownies

1 cup butter (½ pound)
½ cup unsweetened cocoa powder
2 cups sugar
1½ cups all-purpose flour
Pinch of salt
4 eggs
1 teaspoon vanilla

Frosting
¼ cup butter (⅛ pound)
⅓ cup unsweetened cocoa powder
⅓ cup milk
1 teaspoon vanilla
3½ cups confectioners' sugar
½ cup chopped walnuts

Preheat the oven to 350°F. Grease a 15 x 10 x 1-inch jelly roll pan.

In a saucepan, heat the butter and cocoa over low heat until the butter is melted.

Mix the sugar, flour, salt, and eggs. Stir into the butter mixture. Add the vanilla and mix well. Turn into the prepared pan and bake for 20 minutes or until the top springs back when lightly pressed with a finger. Cool on a wire rack.

Meanwhile, prepare the frosting. In a saucepan, heat the butter, cocoa, and milk over low heat until the butter is melted. Add the vanilla and sugar and beat until smooth. Stir in the walnuts.

Frost the brownies while they are still warm, then cut into squares.

***Yield:* 48 brownies**

No-Fuss Chocolate Squares

1½ cups finely crushed graham cracker crumbs
1 (14-ounce) can sweetened condensed milk
1 cup semisweet chocolate chips (6 ounces)
½ cup chopped walnuts
½ teaspoon salt

Preheat the oven to 350°F. Grease well a 9-inch-square baking pan.

Combine all the ingredients in a large bowl. Mix until well blended.

Spread evenly in the prepared pan and bake for 20 minutes or until lightly browned.

Cool on a wire rack and cut into squares.

Yield: 24 squares

Outrageous Peanut Butter Squares

This recipe was created by assistant innkeeper Kathy Moore, who has skillfully prepared nearly every dish in this book hundreds of times.

1¼ cups all-purpose flour
1¼ cups confectioners' sugar
½ cup unsweetened cocoa powder
¾ cup butter
½ cup peanut butter

FILLING

8 ounces softened cream cheese
1 (14-ounce) can sweetened condensed milk
1 egg
2 teaspoons vanilla
1 cup peanut butter chips (6 ounces)

TOPPING

1 teaspoon vegetable oil
½ cup chocolate chips, melted (3 ounces)

Preheat the oven to 350°F. Grease a 13 x 9 x 2-inch baking pan.

Mix the flour, sugar, and cocoa. Cut in the butter and peanut butter with a pastry blender or two knives. Press into the prepared baking pan and bake for 15 minutes.

Meanwhile, make the filling. Mix the cream cheese, milk, egg, and vanilla. Spread over the baked crust. Sprinkle the peanut butter chips over the top and bake for an additional 20 minutes or until lightly browned. Cool on a wire rack.

To make the topping, mix the oil and melted chocolate chips until smooth. Spread over the baked, cooled filling. Cut into squares once the topping is firm.

***Yield:** 36 squares*

Toffee Squares

1 cup butter (½ pound)
1 cup light brown sugar
2 egg yolks
2 cups all-purpose flour
1 teaspoon vanilla
½ cup semisweet chocolate chips (3 ounces)
1 cup finely chopped walnuts

Preheat the oven to 350°F. Grease a 15 x 10 x 1-inch jelly roll pan.

Cream the butter and sugar. Beat in the egg yolks. Add the flour and vanilla and mix well. Spread in the prepared pan and bake for 15 – 20 minutes or until golden.

Melt the chocolate chips and spread over the base while it is still hot. Sprinkle with the walnuts.

Cool on a wire rack and cut into squares.

Yield: 36 squares

Almond Squares

Base
2 eggs
1 cup sugar
1 cup all-purpose flour
1 cup butter, melted (½ pound)

Topping
½ cup butter (¼ pound)
½ cup sugar
½ cup sliced almonds
1 tablespoon all-purpose flour
1 tablespoon milk
1 teaspoon almond extract

Preheat the oven to 350°F. Grease and flour a 13 x 9 x 2-inch baking pan.

Beat the eggs and the sugar with an electric mixer. Stir in the flour and the butter. Turn into the prepared pan and bake for 30 minutes or until lightly browned.

Meanwhile, make the topping. Combine the butter, sugar, almonds, flour, milk, and almond extract in a small saucepan. Cook over low heat, stirring constantly, until thickened.

Spread the topping over the base. Broil 4 inches from the source of heat for a few minutes or until golden brown and bubbly.

Cool on a wire rack and cut into squares.

Yield: 36 squares

Cranberry-Date Squares

2 cups all-purpose flour
2 cups large-flake rolled oats
1½ cups brown sugar
½ teaspoon baking soda
¼ teaspoon salt
1 cup butter, melted (½ pound)
1 (12-ounce) package fresh cranberries
2 cups chopped dates
1 teaspoon vanilla

GLAZE
2 cups confectioners' sugar
½ teaspoon vanilla
2 – 3 tablespoons orange juice

Preheat the oven to 350°F. Grease a 13 x 9 x 2-inch baking pan.

In a large bowl, combine the flour, rolled oats, sugar, baking soda, and salt. Stir in the butter until blended. Pat half the mixture onto the bottom of the prepared baking pan and bake for 8 minutes.

Combine the cranberries and dates in a medium saucepan. Cover and cook over low heat, stirring frequently, for 10 – 15 minutes or until the cranberries pop. Stir in the vanilla.

Carefully spread the cranberry mixture over the crust. Sprinkle the remaining flour mixture on top. Pat down gently. Bake for 20 – 22 minutes or until golden. Cool on a wire rack.

To make the glaze, in a medium bowl mix the sugar, vanilla, and enough orange juice to make a glaze of drizzling consistency.

Drizzle the glaze over the cooled base before cutting it into squares.

Yield:* 36 *squares

Buttermilk-Orange Cupcakes

½ cup softened butter or margarine (¼ pound)
1 cup sugar
2 eggs
2 cups all-purpose flour
1 teaspoon baking soda
¼ teaspoon salt
⅔ cup buttermilk

GLAZE
Juice of 2 oranges
Juice of 2 lemons
1 cup sugar

Preheat the oven to 350°F. Grease 60 miniature muffin cups.

Cream the butter and sugar. Beat in the eggs one at a time.

Combine the flour, baking soda, and salt and stir into the butter mixture alternately with the buttermilk.

Fill the prepared cups less than half full and bake for 8 – 10 minutes or until a wooden toothpick inserted in the center comes out clean.

Meanwhile, make the glaze. Heat the orange juice, lemon juice, and sugar until the sugar is dissolved.

Spoon 1 teaspoon of the glaze over each baked cupcake while it is still in the cup. Let the cupcakes cool in the cups, then remove them.

Serve warm or cold.

***Yield:* 60 miniature cupcakes**

Black-Bottom Cupcakes

1½ cups all-purpose flour
1 teaspoon baking soda
½ teaspoon salt
¼ cup unsweetened cocoa powder
1½ cups sugar
1 cup water
⅓ cup vegetable oil
1 tablespoon vinegar
1 tablespoon vanilla
8 ounces softened cream cheese
1 egg
⅛ teaspoon salt
1 cup semisweet chocolate mini-morsels (6 ounces)

Preheat the oven to 350°F. Grease or paper-line 60 miniature muffin cups.

In a large bowl, combine the flour, baking soda, salt, cocoa, and 1 cup of the sugar. Make a well in the center of the mixture.

Combine the water, oil, vinegar, and vanilla. Pour this into the center of the flour mixture, then stir well. Spoon the batter into the prepared muffin cups, filling each two thirds full.

Combine the cream cheese, egg, salt, and remaining ½ cup of sugar, stirring well. Stir in the chocolate morsels. Spoon 1 teaspoon of this mixture over each cupcake.

Bake for 10 – 15 minutes or until a toothpick inserted in the center comes out clean. Cool on wire racks.

Yield: 60 miniature cupcakes

Cheese Cupcakes

12 round vanilla wafers
1 pound cream cheese
¾ cup sugar
2 eggs
1 tablespoon vanilla
Fresh blueberries
Sliced fresh strawberries

Preheat the oven to 375°F. Paper-line 12 muffin cups and place 1 vanilla wafer in each.

Blend the cream cheese, sugar, eggs, and vanilla. Fill each muffin cup to the brim and bake for 20 minutes or until a wooden toothpick inserted in the center comes out barely moist. Cool on a wire rack.

Top each cupcake with the blueberries and the strawberry slices.

Note: These should be stored in the refrigerator in a tightly sealed container.

Yield: 12 cupcakes

Oatmeal Fruit Tarts

¾ cup butter
1¼ cups light brown sugar
1 egg
⅓ cup milk
1½ teaspoons vanilla
3 cups quick-cooking rolled oats
1 cup all-purpose flour
½ teaspoon baking soda
½ teaspoon salt
¼ teaspoon ground cinnamon
1 cup whole-berry cranberry sauce, cherry pie filling, or fresh blueberries

Preheat the oven to 350°F. Grease 48 miniature muffin cups.

Combine the butter, sugar, egg, milk, and vanilla in a large bowl. Using an electric mixer set at medium speed, beat until well blended.

Combine the rolled oats, flour, baking soda, salt, and cinnamon. Mix into the butter mixture at low speed until just blended.

Shape the dough by the heaping teaspoonful into balls and drop into the prepared muffin cups. Bake for 10 – 12 minutes or until lightly browned. Do not overbake.

While still warm, press the center of each muffin with the handle of a wooden spoon to form a depression. Fill with the cranberry sauce.

Cool completely on a wire rack before removing from the muffin cups.

Yield:* *48 tarts

Thus the fun continues,
Morning, noon, and night,
Till our aching eyelids
Ask for a respite;
Then we soundly slumber
Till the break of day,
Only to again resume
The frolics at Cape May.

Seasonal & Holiday Menus

New Year's Day Brunch

Dreamsicle Oranges (page 26)

Western Oven Omelet (page 40)

Baked Pork Sausage for a Crowd (page 63)

Cranberry-Walnut Scones (page 84)

Apricot Coffee Cake (page 102)

Valentine's Day Tea

Feta Cheese Cups (page 131)

Cheese and Olive Spread (page 141)

Stained-Glass Heart Cookies (page 151)

Fruity Chocolate Dream Bars (page 160)

Fresh Fruit Platter

St. Patrick's Day Brunch

St. Paddy's Day Fruit Medley (page 31)

Potato Quiche (page 58)

Cooked Bacon

Angel Biscuits (page 80), cut into shamrock shapes

Oatmeal Coffee Cake (page 120)

Tulip Festival Tea

Watercress Sandwiches (page 125)

Miniature Quiches (page 133)

Banana-Chocolate Bread (page 74)

Ambrosia Cookies (page 148)

Raisin-Walnut Shortbread Bars (page 155)

Fourth of July Buffet Brunch

Minted Melon (page 30)

Fresh Corn Quiche (page 57)

Sliced Cooked Ham

Lemon-Blueberry Cake (page 107)

Fruit Pizza (page 24)

Tea on the Lawn

Creamy Lemon-Pecan Sandwiches (page 122)

Cheese-Straw Daisy Crackers (page 130)

Layered Pesto Spread (page 144)

California Blondies (page 164)

Black-Bottom Cupcakes (page 179)

Labor Day Picnic Brunch

Poached Apples (page 18)

Fruit Kabobs (page 23)

Pecan Cornbread (page 72)

Blueberry-Nut Bread (page 73)

Peachy Oat Muffins (page 85)

Halloween Late-Night Buffet

Hot Fruit Compote (page 11)

Creamy Scrambled Eggs (page 42)

Apple-Sausage Ring (page 65)

Cheese Muffins (page 91)

Pumpkin Streusel Coffee Cake (page 116)

Christmas Day Brunch

Broiled Grapefruit (page 10)

Eggnog French Toast with Cranberry Syrup (page 37)

Baked Pork Sausage for a Crowd (page 63)

Christmas Tree Bread (page 78)

Whole Wheat Toast, cut into star shapes

Rosy Apple Butter (page 80)

Yuletide Afternoon Tea

Miniature BLT Sandwiches (page 128)

Walnut-Date Cheese Ball (page 136), with crackers and red and green apple slices

Christmas Cheese Spread (page 143)

Easiest Sugar Cookies (page 149)

Christmas Wreath Cookies (page 152)

Oatmeal Fruit Tarts (page 181)

Tips for Cooking & Entertaining

Cooking Tips

Equipping Yourself

ꝏ Before beginning work on a recipe, have all the ingredients set out on the counter. Also, set out any special utensils and equipment such as a juicer, grater, or springform pan.

ꝏ To save steps in the kitchen, buy extra sets of measuring cups and spoons and leave them in the containers you use most often. Keep a cup in the flour bin and the sugar bin and a teaspoon in the baking powder can.

ꝏ Before measuring honey, molasses, or syrup, spray the measuring cup with baking spray. The syrup will slide right out.

ꝏ An ordinary ice cream scoop with a good spring mechanism has several uses. It's perfect for measuring vegetable shortening: 1 scoop equals ¼ cup. Or use it to scoop batter into muffin cups.

Baking Beautifully

ꝏ You'll find it easier to make piecrust if the ingredients are cool. Also, the crust will be flakier if it is chilled before baking. To prevent the bottom from becoming soggy, prick the crust with a fork in several places and sprinkle with 1 tablespoon of flour.

ꝏ For a tall, light muffin, the batter should be a bit lumpy. Over-beating muffin batter results in heavy muffins with air pockets baked in.

ꝏ Muffins will slide out easily if the hot pan is first placed on a wet towel.

ꝏ Sifting flour is time-consuming. To aerate flour, stir it a bit in the canister with a whisk, in case it has become compacted. Lightly spoon the flour into the measuring cup and level off the top with a knife. Other dry ingredients such as baking powder, baking soda, and salt can then be stirred into it.

ꝏ Quick breads are often more flavorful the day after they are baked.

ꝏ If you crave your favorite drop cookie but are short of time, remember that nearly every drop cookie recipe, including chocolate chip, can be baked in a pan as a bar cookie in much less time. Here's how to make elegant diamond-shaped bar cookies: With the pan placed horizontally in front of you, cut the cookie from the top left corner of your rectangular pan toward the lower right corner at a 45-degree angle. Next, cut vertically from the top of the pan to the bottom. The width of your cuts should be consistent (about 1 inch).

Dealing with Dairy Products

ꝏ Egg whites freeze beautifully in ice-cube trays or small plastic bags. To achieve greater volume, bring the egg whites to room temperature before you whip them.

ꝏ Cream will whip more quickly if the cream, bowl, and beaters are chilled.

ꝏ To cream butter and sugar more quickly, first rinse the bowl with hot water.

ꝏ If a recipe calls for buttermilk and you have none on hand, add 1 tablespoon of vinegar to 1 cup of milk and let it stand for 5 minutes.

ꝏ Low-fat dairy products can be successfully substituted for whole-milk products in most recipes. However, there's no substitute for the flavor of real butter in cookie recipes.

Preparing Fruit

ꝏ To ensure that they retain their fresh appearance, dip cut-up fruits that discolor quickly, such as apples, peaches, pears, and bananas, in orange juice.

ꝏ Mash overripe bananas and mix in a little lemon juice. Freeze in measured amounts for later use in banana bread or muffins.

ꝏ You'll get more juice from a lemon if you roll it back and forth on the counter a few times, while pressing firmly with the palm of your hand.

ꕥ Before juicing lemons or oranges, grate the zest, even if the recipe doesn't call for it. Grated lemon and orange zest will keep indefinitely in your freezer, saving you a step later on.

ꕥ To easily remove the peel and white membrane, soak oranges in boiling water for 5 minutes. To skin a tomato, cut an X in the bottom and soak in boiling water for up to 2 minutes.

ꕥ To prepare a mango: Make a single slice, parallel to the long, flat seed, on each side, to halve. Holding the peel side of one half, score the flesh of the mango lengthwise, then crosswise, without cutting through the peel. Bend the scored portion backward and cut close to the peel to loosen the cubed fruit. Cut the peel off the fruit that remains on the seed, then cut off the fruit and dice it.

Toasting Nuts

ꕥ To toast pecans or walnuts, preheat the oven to 350°F. Arrange the nuts closely and evenly on a heavy baking sheet. Bake in the center of the oven for 5 – 7 minutes or until the nuts are a rich golden brown. Spread on paper towels to cool before cutting. You can toast nuts ahead of time and store them in a plastic bag in the freezer.

Tips for Entertaining

ꕥ Don't be a harried host/hostess. Complete every task that is humanly possible before guests arrive. Avoid dishes that need last-minute attention, such as soufflés or temperamental sauces, and anything that requires last-minute frying or whipping.

ꕥ Write detailed reminders to yourself, indicating exactly which dishes are to be served and at what time each should go into the oven and be removed from the oven. Consult this list often, and set timers if necessary.

ꕥ Always have soft music playing in the background before your guests arrive. Music will help them relax and will also fill embarrassing lulls in the conversation.

ꝏ If guests aren't well acquainted, set the dining table with decorative name cards. Placecard holders can be purchased in many attractive styles. Write the guest's name on both sides of the card so those across the table can easily read it.

ꝏ Use unusual and decorative antique serving pieces. Guests enjoy fanciful Victorian silver-plated baskets and serving spoons. Tea served from a beautiful antique teapot seems to taste more delicious! Even milk for cereal seems special when served in an antique milk bottle or a pretty cut-glass pitcher.

ꝏ Keep a record of dishes you serve on each occasion, the guests you entertain, and whether each dish is successful. This way, there's no danger of repeating your mistakes, or of serving the same meal to a guest a second or third time.

ꝏ Serve foods with wide appeal. Avoid serving too many fancy or exotic foods on any one occasion. Unless you know your guests well, serve meat as a side dish in deference to vegetarians.

ꝏ If you're entertaining many guests for tea, serve finger foods exclusively. It's difficult for guests to balance a cup and saucer while handling cutlery. For the sake of your tablecloth and carpet, avoid serving foods that drip or crumble or have bones or shells.

ꝏ Garnish plates of tea sandwiches or cheese spreads with grapes and strawberries. The effect is attractive and there'll be something for serious dieters to nibble.

ꝏ Tea sandwiches prepared in advance can be kept fresh for several hours simply by keeping them well covered. Arrange sandwiches on a serving plate and cover with a dampened dish cloth or paper towel. Cover fully with plastic wrap and refrigerate.

ꝏ Use small cookie and vegetable cutters to make unusual garnishes. Cut stars, hearts, flowers, and animals out of sliced cantaloupe or honeydew melon. Try cutting garnishes out of beets, sweet potatoes, red and green peppers, or whole pimentos. Slices of hard or semi-soft cheese can be cut into attractive shapes and served with crackers.

ꝏ Use large cookie cutters to cut bread for toast into special shapes for holidays. We make heart-shaped toast and biscuits for Valentine's Day and star-shaped toast for Christmas. We even use a turkey-shaped cutter to make toast at Thanksgiving.

ꕤ Found in specialty produce markets or supermarkets carrying gourmet produce, edible flowers such as nasturtiums and pansies make beautiful garnishes for cookie trays or breakfast plates. A purple pansy placed in the center of a half grapefruit or on a slice of melon is always appreciated.

ꕤ Buy inexpensive potted mums from a grocery and cut them for use in your centerpiece. These are much less expensive, and often fresher, than cut flowers from a florist.

ꕤ For the Christmas holidays buy inexpensive poinsettias, no matter how leggy or misshapen they look. Poinsettias make excellent cut flowers and can be kept fresh in bowls and vases for up to 2 weeks. When they're arranged with holiday greens, the results can be striking.

ꕤ Cut flowers will keep longer if you add a little lemon-lime soda to the water.

ꕤ Tuck packets of sachet in drawers or cupboards where you store table linens. Your guests will love the pleasant, fresh fragrance of your napkins and tablecloths.

ꕤ For the holidays, or any special occasion, fill your house with a wonderful spicy fragrance by following this recipe:

4 cups pineapple juice
4 cups water
4 cups apple cider
4 pieces crystallized ginger
3 (3-inch) cinnamon sticks
16 whole cloves
1 teaspoon ground allspice
1 – 2 teaspoons pickling spice

Combine all the ingredients in a large kettle. Boil for a few minutes, then simmer over low heat. (Remember, this recipe is not for consumption!)

Index

D

E

F

G

H

Metric Equivalents

Weight:

1 ounce = 28 grams
1 pound = 454 grams

Volume:

1 teaspoon = 5 milliliters
1 tablespoon = 15 milliliters
¼ cup = 60 milliliters
⅓ cup = 80 milliliters
½ cup = 120 milliliters
⅔ cup = 160 milliliters
1 cup = 230 milliliters

Oven Temperatures:

300°F = 150°C
325°F = 165°C
350°F = 175°C
375°F = 190°C
400°F = 200°C
425°F = 220°C
450°F = 230°C
475°F = 245°C

General Formula for Metric Conversion

- **ounces to grams:** multiply ounce figure by 28.35 to get number of grams
- **grams to ounces:** multiply gram figure by .035 to get number of ounces
- **pounds to grams:** multiply pound figure by 453.59 to get number of grams
- **pounds to kilograms:** multiply pound figure by 0.45 to get number of kilograms
- **ounces to milliliters:** multiply ounce figure by 30 to get number of milliliters
- **cups to liters:** multiply cup figure by 0.24 to get number of liters
- **Fahrenheit to Celsius:** subtract 32 from the Fahrenheit figure, multiply by 5, then divide by 9 to get Celsius figure
- **Celsius to Fahrenheit**: multiply Celsius figure by 9, divide by 5, then add 32 to get Fahrenheit figure
- **inches to centimeters:** multiply inch figure by 2.54 to get number of centimeters
- **centimeters to inches:** multiply centimeter figure by 0.39 to get number of inches

About the Author

Sue Carroll was among the first bed & breakfast proprietors in the country. A former teacher, she has been a professional innkeeper/chef since 1971 and has become an expert on Victoriana and house restoration and decorating techniques as well as breakfast, brunch, and tea entertaining.

Sue Carroll's prize-winning recipes have appeared in *Bon Appetit* and numerous travel magazines. She has demonstrated menu highlights and shared cooking tips on local and national television, including the popular PBS series *Inn Country USA*.

Contact the Mainstay Inn at:

635 Columbia Avenue
Cape May, New Jersey 08204
Tel: (609) 884-8690